Hooking Fine Gifts

16 Projects for Rug Hookers

Happy DiFranza and Steve DiFranza

STACKPOLE
BOOKS

Published by
STACKPOLE BOOKS
Cameron and Kelker Streets
P.O. Box 1831
Harrisburg, PA 17105

Cover photo by Mel Goldman
Cover design by Caroline Miller

Printed in the United States of America

First Edition

10 9 8 7 6 5 4 3 2 1

Library of Congress Cataloging-in-Publication Data

DiFranza, Happy.
    Hooking fine gifts : 16 projects for rug hookers / Happy DiFranza
and Steve DiFranza.
      p.   cm.
    Includes index.
    ISBN 0-8117-2545-6
    1. Hooking. I. DiFranza, Steve. II. Title.
TT833.D54   1992
746.4—dc20   92-11863
                                      CIP

To our daughters, Elizabeth and Suzanne,
and to our son-in-law, Joseph Petretta,
for their enduring and patient support

Contents

Acknowledgments

First mention must be given to Ethel Bruce, ever encouraging and never constraining, who showed us that rug hooking can be an exciting adventure. Our daughters, Elizabeth and Suzanne, helped hook the models, and we are grateful for their thoughtful and conscientious assistance. Our son-in-law, Joseph Petretta, gave invaluable technical guidance; our nephew, Paul Amante, was always patient in overseeing the smooth operation of our equipment; and our brother-in-law, Frank Amante, stood ready to assist with construction of a fireboard. Questions about wool were always carefully answered by Terry Dorr. Mel Goldman has generously advised us on the photography. Anne Ashworth and Marcy VanRoosen offered wise counsel on the scope of the book. For help with conservation techniques, we are most indebted to Elizabeth Lahikainen, Head Upholstery Conservator at the Conservation Center of the Society for the Preservation of New England Antiquities, and to her assistant, Karen Myrholm. Grateful appreciation is also extended to our editor, Toni Albert.

Introduction

Rug hooking, which evolved from the needlework tradition of the mid-nineteenth century, uses an easily mastered technique of looping narrow fabric strips through a backing, but the simplicity of the technique hasn't limited experimentation in color and design. Traditionally, hooked rugs were not created as "art." They were fashioned out of woolen scraps to serve as practical floor coverings, and they were made by women who would probably not have given their time to painting or to some other art form. But hooked rugs often reflect a sophisticated understanding of form and color. The beauty and craftsmanship of hooked pieces have finally led to their being acknowledged as a significant part of the American folk art tradition.

Steve and I became enthusiastic about rug hooking over thirty years ago when we purchased our first home and, like our nineteenth-century ancestors, needed rugs for the floor. Our combined training in art history and design propelled us toward developing our own hooked rug patterns, and we have enjoyed focusing on a contemporary approach to the craft. Steve, with eight years of education in drawing, painting, and design, has supplied the ideas, artwork, and photography for this book. My academic background placed me in the position of researching and writing the book (as well as manufacturing the hooked pieces).

The projects presented here are an outgrowth of our shared experience. We have borrowed traditional forms, such as chair seats, brick covers, and rugs, but we have also included wall pieces, pillows, and a fireboard, since the rug hooking technique can obviously be used for more than utilitarian items. With discretionary time at such a minimum today, the projects were designed to be completed within a reasonable time without appearing minimal. Options are given for those who wish to accomplish a project easily by using what is immediately at hand. For people who wish to experience the full range of skills associated with rug hooking, complete directions are given. For each project, a line drawing in a grid is provided as a pattern that can be enlarged. Commercial patterns for each project may be obtained from DiFranza Designs. (See Sources of Supply at the back of the book.)

We hope you will enjoy the challenge and pleasure of hooking fine gifts for your family and friends.

How to Hook

Getting Ready to Hook

Hooking Is Easy

When people see me working on a rug hooking project, they often comment, "It looks so easy!" And indeed it *is* easy. Everyone can pull cut-up fabric strips through a backing to make a pile, and everyone can hook. Certainly no unusual physical strength is needed, so it is an appropriate activity for most people. Given a clear explanation, a person can learn how to hook on the first try and, with practice, can soon be working easily and confidently.

Experience with other needlework forms, even sewing, is not a prerequisite for hooking rugs. Rug hooking is much less demanding than most other needlework; it accommodates a variety of techniques and materials with equal success. Those who claim to have no ability with their hands often become the most avid rug hookers. Even less-than-perfect eyesight is not a deterrent, since once the hooking motion becomes automatic, much of the work is done by the sense of touch.

It won't matter if you haven't had formal training in color and design. Your taste has already been conditioned by exposure to various decorative media. The color choices you've made when selecting clothes and furnishings are the same kinds of decisions you will make when choosing a design and a color scheme for a rug, so you've already had practice thinking creatively. You will develop new abilities—a new eye for color and design—as you work on various projects.

An attractive aspect of rug hooking, particularly for today's lifestyle, is the ease of setup. Your project can be left in a corner or stored in a closet, where it is quickly available when you decide to hook. It is never necessary to complete a particular phase at one sitting. You might make a few loops while the potatoes boil, or you might work for several hours. Interruptions are never hazardous to the success of your project.

Hooking Is Fun

When you ask people why they like to hook, they often say that it is relaxing. There seems to be something soothing in the technique of looping strips of fabric through a backing. Since this process doesn't always require your complete attention, you can watch television, listen to music, or have a conversation while you work.

Some people find that working on a hooking project is company enough, and they work happily in solitude. Others don't hook at all unless they're with a group of friends, enjoying the camaraderie of exchanging praise and advice. Classes often supply the opportunity to be sociable, as well as offer a source of inspiration. As in earlier times, hooking bees are still held, eagerly anticipated as social events complete with heavy laden tables.

Hooking Is Inexpensive

My favorite hooking time is early in the morning with my second cup of coffee.

The origin of rug hooking is not precisely known, but the craft gained great popularity during the mid-1800s, when burlap and woolen fabric, the primary materials in hooked rugs, became readily available. Textile mills turned out quantities of woolen materials, providing household fabrics—and scraps to save—in great abundance. More important, jute was imported from Asia and woven into burlap, a sturdy fabric with an open weave,

Basic equipment. A pattern is ready to be stretched on a simple 14-inch hoop or a 14-inch hoop on a stand. The addition of a long bolt at the thumbscrew allows for extra expansion. Other items needed for hooking are a hook, scissors, and strips of wool fabric.

which was used to make feed and grain sacks. When opened at the seams, burlap bags could be used as backings for hearth rugs or doormats, decorative items that were considered very fashionable in American homes of the period. The open-weave burlap made it easy to loop fabric strips to make a pile, and tools from the needlework tradition, such as crochet hooks or button hooks, were easily adapted for that purpose. If a frame were used, it could be readily made from scrap lumber.

Since the essential tools were so simple, rug hooking was a craft everyone could do. The unfettered process gave free rein to the maker's fancy, and the transformation of waste materials into something beautiful appealed to everyone's sense of thrift. This is still true today.

Hooking Requires Little Basic Equipment

The equipment required in the nineteenth century to hook a rug is still the only equipment needed today. There are only a few essentials:

- A backing with outline design
- Woolen material cut into strips
- A frame for stretching the backing
- A hook
- Scissors

Ordinary tweezers are handy for removing wool strips if you need to change a color or rework an area.

Early hooked rugs were made by using what was at hand, and the choices were limited. Today, as rug hooking has become a more conscious art form, more options are available. Burlap competes with monk's cloth, rug warp, and linen as backing material. Used clothing, which can be dismantled and cut into strips, can be gathered at secondhand stores, rummage sales, and flea markets. Sometimes the scrap bins in fabric stores yield a choice piece of woolen material. But to meet the demand for wool flannel, which is the best fabric to use for rug hooking, retailers have made it available by the yard in a wide range of colors. Flannel also comes in precut strips, ready for the hook.

The standing frame of the early 1900s is seldom seen today; it has been replaced by smaller and more portable hoops and lap frames. Hooks can be purchased in several sizes with a variety of turned handles. Ordinary scissors will always serve when you need to snip an end, but there are more convenient styles with offset handles and tiny clippers that make close cutting very easy.

The discussion that follows will help the beginner collect what is needed to make a hooked rug and will encourage the experienced rug maker to try some new directions. Rug hooking offers great freedom of individual expression. Choosing a design and planning the colors can be an exhilarating experience, especially when we are assured that whatever the outcome, there is no such thing as a bad hooked rug.

Choosing a Fabric for the Backing

A variety of fabrics can be used as a backing or foundation for hooking. Some are more readily available than others; some are more durable. To choose the right backing, consider what you are going to make, what you prefer to work on, and the width of the strips you plan to use. A more closely woven backing can be used with fine strips. Wide strips require a more open weave.

Burlap

The traditional and most widely used backing for rug hooking is burlap, or jute cloth. The open weave makes it easy to pull up the fabric strips, and it has a pleasant firmness that allows for even stretching. Burlap has always been an inexpensive fabric. Sold in 40-, 48-, and 60-inch widths, it comes in both fine and coarse weaves. They are identified by thread weight; the finer is called 12- or 13-ounce burlap, and the coarser is called 10-ounce burlap. The fine weave is suitable for narrow $3/32$-inch or $1/8$-inch strips, and the 10-ounce burlap is used for strips $5/32$ inch to $1/4$ inch or wider.

To loosen the weave of a backing fabric, you can pull threads at a selected interval.

Monk's Cloth

Monk's cloth is 100 percent cotton. It was widely used during World War II, when burlap was hard to get. The two-by-two weave (two warp threads and two weft threads) is most suitable for hooking. Light-colored, soft, and pliable, monk's cloth accommodates both narrow and wide strips. It is also available in widths up to 144 inches, so a room-sized rug can be hooked on this backing without seaming.

Rug Warp

This is also 100 percent cotton. Heavier than monk's cloth, rug warp is a white fabric with a simple, even weave, available in widths from 56 inches to 244 inches. It can be used for narrow strips as well as for strips up to $3/16$ inch wide, but wider strips are difficult to pull up. Large projects can be accommodated without piecing.

Linen

Although some early hooked rugs were made on linen backings, this backing is a relative newcomer. The linen, or tow cloth, used in the old rugs was rather closely woven, making it necessary to punch holes as the strips were pulled through. The linen that is available today is more coarsely woven and accommodates a range of strip widths from narrow to wide. Its light color makes the outline design very readable, and its firmness makes it easy to stretch and to hook on. It comes in both 48-inch and 60-inch widths. The most expensive foundation fabric, it is also the most durable.

Wool Homespun

Wool homespun is a loosely woven woolen fabric that can nicely accommodate hooking. Its light weight makes it inappropriate for rugs, but it makes an attractive backing for a pillow or wall hanging if you plan to work only the design and leave the backing unhooked as a background. The design has a very attractive embossed appearance after being hooked, because the homespun backing is soft. Like monk's cloth, it is pliable, and the weave generally requires a fine strip. Usually, homespun is 60 inches wide.

Wool homespun is a remnant or a second of upholstery fabric, so unfortunately, the supply is erratic.

Natural Fibers and Synthetics

All of the backings discussed so far have weaves that facilitate making a looped pile. Some will accommodate a wider range of strip widths than others, so when you choose a backing, it is important to know what strip width you are going to use. Also, all of the backings mentioned are natural fibers, which I prefer. Occasionally, I have seen someone working on a synthetic backing, but no research has been done to evaluate how well synthetics work as foundations for hooked, woolen pile. Until more facts are available, natural fibers are a more reliable choice.

Enlarging, Transferring, and Edging the Design

Enlarging a Design by Hand

Enlarging a design from this book is not hard to do. It is a purely technical process. You will need the following items:

- Paper for your enlargement
- Pencil
- Ruler
- Black marker with a fine point

Each project design has a grid already drawn on it. Each square on the grid represents a 2-inch square on the enlarged pattern. First decide what size your finished project will be. Then select a piece of paper large enough to accommodate the full size of your project, and use a black marker to mark it into squares. If you wish to make your project the same size as the model, draw a grid with 2-inch squares. If you wish to make your project half the size of the model, draw 1-inch squares. If you want your project to be twice the size of the model, draw 4-inch squares. Put consecutive numbers in the corners of the squares on your grid and add the same numbers to the grid in the book. To keep your design in proportion, the number of squares in your grid must be the same as the number of squares in the grid in the book. This numbering system will also help you check your work as you carefully copy the details of the design onto your paper.

Enlarging a Design by Machine

If you have access to a commercial printer with a sophisticated photocopier or a photostat camera, you can have an enlargement done for you. A business offering reprographic services for architects will also perform this service.

Transferring the Design from the Paper

After enlarging your design, the next step is to transfer it to your backing fabric. You will need the following materials:

• Backing fabric large enough to allow a 4-inch working area beyond the margin of your design

• Red Dot Tracer or bridal tulle

• Black marker with a fine point

• Common pins

Red Dot Tracer is a white filament material available in fabric stores for copying patterns. Printed with a red dot grid at 1-inch intervals, it works as a handy guide for keeping your work straight. It is only 45 inches wide, but you can put pieces together if your project is very large. If this product is not available, you can use bridal tulle as an alternative.

With a marker, trace your enlargement onto the filament. Center this over your backing fabric, pinning it securely. Trace over your design with the marker, working slowly and using firm pressure so that the ink will bleed through. It may be necessary to darken some lines afterward.

Hooked pieces, particularly rugs, often have the initials of the maker and the date worked into the design.

Edging the Pattern

Unless you finish the raw edges of your pattern, it will ravel unpleasantly as you work. Make a narrow hem at the edge or cover it with masking tape.

Choosing Fabric for the Strips

Woolen fabric has always been associated with hooked rugs. Indeed, the popularity of rug hooking in the mid-nineteenth century paralleled the mechanical production of woolen material, which made wool for hooked rugs readily available. Although cotton and silk are sometimes found in old rugs, their soil resistance and durability are inferior to those of wool. Of course, not all woolen material is usable; the weave and the weight of the fabric determine whether it can be used for hooking.

All-Wool Flannel

In the early twentieth century, hundreds of mills turned out woolen cloth, and scrap fabric was readily available and inexpensive. This is no longer true.

Wool flannel is the nicest kind of fabric to use for hooking because it is pliable and woven finely enough to be cut into narrow strips, as well as wider widths. It can be purchased in 54-, 56-, and 60-inch widths. If you are cutting up old clothes, wool flannel would be found most often in sports jackets, skirts, and men's bathrobes. Finding this material in white, ivory, and pale pastel shades is particularly valuable, since these colors can easily be overdyed if they are not usable as they are.

Wool Coating and Blankets

Coating material is apt to be heavier than flannel. Some of it is too heavy and feltlike to be used successfully. Some will work for 1/4-inch-wide strips, but other coating material is so loosely woven that it will fall apart when cut in any width. Blankets may not always be usable either, but because they offer such a quantity of material, don't pass them up without thorough examination or testing.

Wool Checks, Tweeds, and Plaids

Wool checks are eagerly sought, especially the tiny pin checks that make such wonderful veins for leaves or accents in flower centers. Of course, 1/8-inch checks can be cut up, too; the result is a bolder accent. One-half-inch checks are apt to produce a blotchy appearance when hooked in, but they can be successfully overdyed. Weaves vary, so examine them with your strip width in mind.

Tweeds give an attractive, peppered texture when hooked. Like checks, the bolder weaves work as accents. If they are subtle, tweeds can be mixed in solid-color backgrounds to add interest. They are too dominating to be used alone for a background.

Small plaids are more usable than large blocks of color, but sometimes sections of a bold plaid can be used to achieve just the effect you need. Of course, large plaids can be overdyed to produce interesting results.

Paisley Shawls

These multicolored, woven shawls can sometimes be picked up inexpensively in antiques shops if the fabric is not in perfect condition. Made of fine wool, they make wonderful accents when hooked in. They add rather intense touches, however, so they are not usually used in quantity. They must be cut by hand in strips at least 1/4 inch wide.

Wool Blends

With the price of wool escalating all the time, textile mills are producing more woolen fabrics with synthetic components. Some merchants are now advertising wool blends for hooking. If the synthetic content is small, you probably won't perceive any difference between a wool blend and 100 percent wool. However, synthetic fibers will dull your scissors or cutter head faster. Also, if you dye the fabric, the results may not be what you anticipated.

There are two simple experiments to determine whether material is 100 percent wool. If the fabric turns to ash when you hold a lighted match to the edge, it is wool. If it balls up, it contains synthetics. Another test is to put a small swatch of fabric in pure bleach. After an hour, the 100 percent woolen fabric will have disintegrated; the blend will remain. Of course, neither of these tests can be made at the point of sale, but they are useful to confirm any doubts you may have.

Other factors to bear in mind if you use blends in any quantity are their soil resistance and durability. Synthetics tend to hold soil, and they wear at a different rate from the wool fibers.

Scraps and Old Clothes

Using scraps, or pound goods, and cutting up old clothes appeal to the sense of thrift in all of us, and scavenging in secondhand stores and at rummage sales can yield real treasures for hooking. Heavily worn items should be avoided, of course. And straying too far from 100 percent wool is not advisable; check garments for fabric content labels. Before storing the garments, it is best to rip out zippers, linings, and facings, and it is important to wash them, since not all woolens have been mothproofed.

After word gets around that you are hooking rugs, people may bring you materials that they've been hoarding. Never refuse these offerings; what is not usable can always be passed on to charity.

Wool Fabrics Unsuitable for Hooked Rugs

The following list of unsuitable fabrics is offered only as a guide. If a material is the perfect color, hand cutting it or using it double might make it usable.

Twill weaves	Strips fall apart after cutting
Jersey and knits	Unpleasantly stretchy to hook with

Worsted	Too thready to work with
Cashmere	Too soft to be durable
Melton cloth	Too feltlike to work with

Materials for Decorative Hooking

Until fairly recently, the rug hooking technique was employed only to make rugs. Choosing fabrics suitable for floor coverings had to satisfy the practical aspect of use. But as the craft has become a more conscious art, more decorative uses have evolved. If you are making a piece to be hung, or even a pillow top, abrasive wear is not a factor, and aggressive cleaning will not be necessary. For decorative hooking, any fabric that will hang together when cut into strips can be used.

Choosing Colors for Your Project

Importance of Color

Color in hooked pieces is very important; it is what the viewer first responds to. The loops may be meticulous, but unless the colors are interesting and enhance the design, the work will receive only a passing glance. Ideally, a hooked piece should be attractive by itself, as well as work successfully in the area for which it was made, so there is always a double challenge.

Selecting a Color Scheme

Hooked rugs made with fabric strips are not readily available commercially. They are usually made by a homemaker to decorate the home.

When you begin to think about a hooking project, you usually have a specific place in mind that needs decoration. The colors that are already in the room can be a guide. The color schemes used in the draperies and the wallpaper can be repeated, or the upholstery fabric may offer some inspiration. An alternative to matching the colors in a room is to deliberately vary the colors to emphasize closely related hues.

Home decorating magazines offer other suggestions, and pictured room settings may show a color combination that will be perfect for you. Adapting the colors in a bedspread or fabric display may solve the color scheme for your rug or pillow. Perusing an art book and analyzing what painters have chosen can be helpful. A visit to the textile department of your local museum is another source for inspiration. It isn't wrong to copy a color scheme; you will be using it in an entirely different way, and it will change as you work with it, becoming yours in the process.

Choosing a Background Color

Choosing a color for the background is the first decision that you should make. In the early planning stages, all that is needed is to decide on a dark, medium, or light background. Dark backgrounds require fairly bright design motifs. Medium backgrounds must be carefully balanced with the colors in the design, so that the design is strong enough to be clear. Pale backgrounds can support more delicately colored designs, but the edges of the motifs must not blend with the background. As you refine the details of your color choices, the exact background color will fall into focus. It is always a good idea to work the background simultaneously with the design, not only to prevent the boredom of hooking only background, but also to guard against mistaking your foundation color for the background color.

Practical considerations enter into the choice of background color, too. If you are making a welcome rug to be used at an entrance, remember that an off-white background will soil quickly. But such a background is fine in a bedroom or any other area that doesn't have heavy use.

Choosing Colors for the Design

Usually artists work in just three or four colors; what may appear as additional colors are only variants. It is not necessary to incorporate a rainbow of colors in your rug, either. You can do wonders with a very simple palette. It is always a good idea to use a color more than once; using a color three times will achieve a pleasing triangular balance. Sometimes you can do two things at once by using

Mixing two or three close values of a color when hooking the background makes it more interesting.

different values of a color, making it appear both as a repetition and as a color variation.

Perceptual Distortions

The more you use color, the more you will realize that color possesses a life of its own that will assert itself when you're least expecting it. This is particularly apparent when you combine colors, because they affect one another differently. Yellow beside red will appear warmer than yellow beside green. The quantity of yellow, green, and red will be a factor as well. This is why a combination of colors you've mentally conjured up may not work when you actually use them together. For example, a dark field will absorb colors, making them seem less vibrant than they are individually.

Another element that affects color is texture. A color hooked into loops appears slightly darker than it does as a flat piece of wool. This will sometimes trip you up, particularly if you are trying to match something exactly. I no longer try to be too exact, preferring instead to think of slight variations as more interesting.

You really can't think about color without considering the effect of light. A printed surface, such as a colored picture in a magazine, reflects light. A colored sketch of your project worked out with markers does the same thing. On the other hand, a hooked surface is matte and absorbs light. And this is where frustration can set in. Having carefully worked out a color scheme with markers, you find when you translate it to wool that the balance is off; part of the design is too dark and stands out, and another section is too light and recedes.

Graphic artists must constantly deal with this discrepancy when they present designs to clients, so rug hookers are not unique. You will have to make adjustments, knowing beforehand that these differences can arise. Despite this difficulty, I still think it is valuable to fiddle with your color scheme on paper before you take up your hook. You will find this exercise helpful, even though it isn't always perfect. Usually the adjustments that must be made are ones of value, not of color.

A way of getting around this perceptual difficulty is to plan your colors with the wools, assuming you have them on hand. Arranging the colors as you will hook them, side by side and in the approximate proportions in which they will be used, will give you a good idea of the appearance of the finished piece.

Color Vocabulary

There are a number of systems that have been developed for organizing and identifying colors. They are interesting to explore and can help increase your awareness of the dynamics of color. Some of the precise terms that have evolved to describe colors are discussed below.

Color Wheel. The *color wheel* is the simplest and most popular color system. Primary colors—red, blue, and yellow—from which all other colors are made, are placed at equal intervals on the color wheel. The secondary colors—orange, green, and purple—are placed between the primary colors.

Complementary. *Complementary* describes the relationship between colors directly opposite one another on the color wheel. Complementary colors enhance each other. When complements are used in strength, they are riveting. For this reason, they are often used in commercial packaging and billboards. For decorative work, complements must be grayed, but they can still provide a valuable starting point for planning a color scheme. When mixed together, they will darken one another and produce a more interesting color than you would get by adding black. Here are the complementary colors:

- Red and green
- Blue and orange
- Yellow and purple

Hue. *Hue* is a more accurate name for color, referring to its pure, saturated state.

Intensity. *Intensity* refers to the strength or weakness of a color and is sometimes called *chroma*. Colors of high intensity are generally used in small quantities.

Value. The *value* of a color is its lightness or darkness in relation to a gray scale. A black and white photo shows only values. When shading colors, values must be consecutive to produce even transitions. When using values of a color in segments of a motif, they must be distinct enough to be clear when viewed from a distance.

Everyone appreciates color, and most people are affected by it more than they realize. A room decorated with poor color choices may make the occupants uncomfortable. When you choose colors for your project, be aware of your own feelings. If you feel disturbed by a combination, change it. Unless you are convinced that someone else's response is more accurate or more appropriate than yours, follow your own inclinations.

Collecting or Dyeing the Colors You Need

Finding Old Clothes

Traditionally, rug hooking was a scrap craft. Museum collections and the antique trade testify to the great beauty that has been achieved with leftovers. Today, with thoughtful hunting and careful planning, it is still possible to create something unique and attractive using scraps. Secondhand clothing stores offer a good supply of woolens, but they are not as economical as they used to be. Yard sales and rummage sales may yield better bargains. Of course, the scrap tables at fabric stores are always worth checking. Being "into" rug hooking is like being an antiques buff: you're always on the prowl.

To prevent erratic buying, it's a good idea to have a plan in mind as you collect woolens. But it is wise to grab any ivories or pale pastels you find, in case you decide you would like to try dyeing. As you hunt, you should bear in mind that you can alter colors somewhat by boiling them in a little detergent, which causes the colors to bleed. Sometimes a screaming piece can be made usable by doing this. Unfortunately, you can't tell by looking at a

Contrary to popular belief, hooked rugs were not always made for reasons of thrift. They were also made because it is fun to hook.

piece of fabric whether it will bleed, so you have to buy on faith. Using a little ammonia, instead of detergent, will disturb the color of most fabrics, but it is harsh treatment and will leave the wool feeling stiff.

You will need to dismantle any garments that you buy, since zippers, linings, padding, and buttons will be of no use to you. Garments should then be ripped apart and heavily tailored sections and worn areas discarded. Moths don't like clean wool, so take time to wash it.

Woolens By Mail

Fabric for hooking can also be ordered by mail. Scraps by the pound, as well as by the yard, can arrive right at your doorstep. If you don't own a cutter or don't wish to cut strips by hand, precut strips, called stripettes, are available in several widths. There are also sources for hand-dyed and custom-dyed wools, although these usually are not precut. (See Sources of Supply on page 145.)

Dyeing the Colors You Need

Combining wool scraps with new wool can be done effectively, but for many rug hookers, the range of commercial colors is too limiting. For this group, dyeing offers a rainbow of possibilities that is very exciting. Indeed, some become so enchanted that they do more dyeing than hooking. Actually, since natural dyes were used to color early rugs, this skill has always been associated with rug hooking. As commercial dyes became available for home use, ruggers substituted them for the more difficult-to-use natural dyes.

To tighten the weave of a woolen fabric, wash it and put it in the dryer.

Dyeing, as it is practiced by rug hookers, is a simple process, easily handled in a kitchen at home. It can be a very casual procedure, going on while you do other things, since there is no long stirring period or pot watching required. The two-step dyeing process can be interrupted to accommodate your schedule. Indeed, wool can cool in the dyebath, absorbing the last vestiges of color, while you're out. When you return, it can be rinsed and popped in the dryer with a Turkish towel. Something else to remember is that no misstep is ever truly a mistake. If you forget to add something, you can add it later; if the color isn't just what you wanted, it may be the perfect color for a future project.

Selecting the Dye

Rug hookers who use commercial dyes usually work with either ProChem Washfast Dyes or Cushing Perfection Dyes. ProChem dyes are sold in several basic colors in small jars; then the colors must be combined. Cushing dyes, available in ninety-six colors, are sold in small packets. The colors, mixtures of different dyes, can be used right from the package or combined for more subtle effects. Although Cushing dyes are more expensive than the ProChem dyes, I find the Cushing dyes more convenient to use. All directions given are based on Cushing dyes.

It should be mentioned that dyes have a will of their own, no matter what brand or type you're using. When you least expect it, you experience a color variation, even though you've repeated the steps of the process faithfully. For those with exacting temperaments, this is annoying, but it should be viewed as a lesson in learning how to make these slight variations work *for* you. In most cases, these mutations can be fingered into your work. Hooked pieces that have elusive hints of related colors are far more pleasing to the viewer and give your work a personal signature.

Also, the colors you dye will not be perfectly even like those in commercial fabrics, but that unevenness makes them *better* for hooking, adding a liveliness to your work. Upon occasion, you may want to deliberately spot your wools with various colors.

Procedures Common to All Dyeing Processes

There are four procedures used in every dye method:
1. Presoaking the wool.
2. Adding water for the dyebath.
3. Adding a mordant.
4. Heating the dyebath with the wool.

The first step in dyeing is to presoak the wool by covering it with hot water. To assist the wetting process and the subsequent absorption of the dye, you should add a wet-

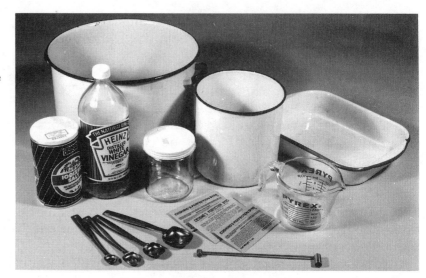

Dye equipment. Packages of Cushing Perfection Dye, a dye spoon, kitchen measuring spoons, storage jars, pans, and a fork are assembled for dyeing. Salt and white vinegar are the simple mordants used to set the dye. Paper towels are handy for keeping the area neat.

ting agent, such as household detergent or Orvus, a better product. (See Maintenance of Hooked Pieces on page 44.) The soaking period can be as short as ten minutes, or you can soak the wool overnight if that is more convenient. Rinse the wool thoroughly after presoaking, particularly if you have used household detergent.

The material being dyed must be covered with water to enable the dye particles to be circulated when the water is heated. The amount of water in the dyebath doesn't matter as long as there is enough water to allow the material you're dyeing to swim easily.

To ensure that the color you have chosen remains permanent, a mordant, or setting agent, is necessary. Both the ProChem dyes and the Cushing dyes can be set with ordinary salt or vinegar. Kosher, iodized, or common salt may be used. White vinegar is usually the most economical and works well.

The kind of mordant used will affect the dye somewhat. When salt is used, the dye penetrates the material slowly; when vinegar is used, the dye is absorbed more quickly. I generally use both salt and vinegar. I add the salt at the beginning of the dye process and about twenty minutes later, I add the vinegar. Using the two mordants produces a better and more even absorption of dye, especially when dyeing deep colors.

It is not necessary to measure the salt or vinegar precisely. I use approximately 1/2 teaspoon of salt for a 2-quart pan, then about 1 tablespoon of vinegar. For a larger, 8-quart pot, which will hold 1/2 yard of wool, I use 1 tablespoon of salt and approximately 1/3 cup of vinegar.

Dye will not penetrate material unless heat is applied. You can use your kitchen range. The entire dyeing process can take from twenty minutes to one hour. Allowing the wool to cool in the dyebath is ideal, since the wool absorbs the last particles of dye during this time.

Equipment for Dyeing

You will need the following equipment for dyeing:

- Dye
- Dye measuring spoon
- Kitchen measuring spoons
- 1-cup jars for holding and storing dissolved dye
- Boiling water
- Paper towels
- 2-quart and 8-quart pans, preferably white enamel
- Salt
- White vinegar
- Long-handled fork for stirring

Most of the supplies needed for dyeing are already part of your household equipment. Any pan can be used for dyeing, but the white or cream surface of an enamel pan makes it easier to judge your color. Enamel cookware is available in some hardware stores, but I scavenge second-hand stores and antiques shops for mine. It doesn't matter if they are chipped, since they won't be used for cooking. (In fact, it is a good idea to set aside equipment for dyeing and use it only for that purpose.)

Dye spoons are very convenient for measuring dry dye, because they have a measure for 1/32 teaspoon on one end and 1/4 teaspoon on the other end. These are the commonly used measurements for dyeing.

Using Dry Dye

Cushing dyes may be used in their powdered form right from the package. Some dyes are stronger than others, so the amount you use will vary. The printed color card indicates dye strengths. Measuring directly from the package is a simple and efficient way to dye 1/3-yard or 1/2-yard pieces when you know you will need this amount of the same color. Usually you use 1/32 teaspoon or 1/4 teaspoon, or multiples of them, depending on the color you want. And, of course, you can combine several dyes. Dipping a wet dye spoon in the dry dye, so that you pick up a coating of dye on the surface, is a handy trick if you want just a tint and if exact duplication isn't necessary.

When adding dry dye to the dyebath, use your fork to pull the wool back, so that the dye falls in the water and not directly on the wool; otherwise, you will get inappropriate spotting.

Dissolving Dye and Mixing Formulas

If you want to use dye in smaller amounts than you can measure with the dye spoon or with kitchen measuring spoons, you must dissolve it in boiling water. Of course, the amount of dye and water can be varied, but a general rule is to use 1/2 teaspoon of dry dye dissolved in 1 cup of boiling water. Measure the dye carefully, even wiping off particles clinging to the spoon. It is important to measure the water precisely, too. Stir thoroughly to make sure all the particles are in the solution.

Once you have made a dye solution, any amount can be measured from this solution. You can make several values of the same color or quantities of a particular value. Generally, doubling the measurement of dye will give you one value deeper. I find the following table useful for dyeing an eight-value gradation of the same color or for dyeing a specific value.

Value 1	1/4 teaspoon (Lightest color)
Value 2	1/2 teaspoon
Value 3	1 teaspoon
Value 4	2 teaspoons
Value 5	4 teaspoons
Value 6	2 tablespoons
Value 7	8 teaspoons
Value 8	4 tablespoons (Darkest color)

Dry dye and dissolved dye may be combined to give subtle and unusual colors. Many dye methods and recipes, called formulas, have been published to help you; a number of booklets detailing procedures are available with accompanying swatches. The ones I use most often:

Ashworth, Anne. *Chroma Craft.* Published by author, 1971.

Ashworth and Armstrong. *Green Mountain Colors.* Green Mountain Rug School, 1989.

Hicks, Lydia. *Triple Over Dye, Book I.* Published by author, 1957.

Procedure for Open-Pan Dyeing

To dye wool in an open pan, first determine the amount of wool you wish to dye, and select a pot that will accommodate it easily. Presoak the material, rinse it, and cover it in the pot with hot tap water. Place the pot on the stove at high heat, and add the dye, either dry or as a solution. Stir with a fork, and bring the water to a boil. Pull the wool aside, add salt, and stir again. Turn the heat to medium and simmer the dyebath for twenty minutes. Add vinegar, stir, and simmer twenty minutes longer. Turn off the heat and allow the wool to cool in the dyebath. Then rinse the wool thoroughly and dry it. Store any unused dye in a tightly covered jar. It will keep indefinitely; if it crystallizes, you can redissolve it.

Dip-Dyeing

Dip-dyeing is the easiest way to achieve perfect shading. If you hook with wide strips, you must use this method to achieve those painterly gradations of color.

It is customary in dip-dyeing to use long, narrow strips of white or pastel wool measuring four times the longest section you wish to shade. You will need a dyebath about 3 inches deep to which you've added dye and 1 tablespoon of vinegar. Wearing a rubber glove on your right hand, hold a presoaked strip over the boiling dyebath. Dip the strip about one-third of the way into the dyebath, always keeping it moving to avoid a color line. When this end is as dark as you wish, dip the strip two-thirds of the way into the dyebath, still keeping it moving. If you wish to give the

The dry outer skins of onions, used to add a golden luster to pastel wools, are stuffed in an old stocking for easy handling. Color from the onion skins is extracted by simmering them. The skins can also be placed between layers of pastel wool to produce a spotted effect.

lightest end a wash of color, dip it very quickly once or twice, or leave the light end undyed.

When a strip is dyed, lay it in a flat pan with 1 inch of simmering water to which 1 tablespoon of vinegar has been added. Additional pieces may be added to the pan, but keep the dark and light ends together. When you've dipped all the strips and put them in the setting pan, cover the pan loosely with foil and simmer for about twenty minutes. Check to make sure the water doesn't boil away. If the wool burns, it will smell terrible and can't be used.

Overdyeing and Spot-Dyeing

Overdyeing is a method of altering the color of commercially dyed fabric. Overdyeing can transform a frog into a prince by creating new, subtle colorings. Any loud color can be muted by giving it a wash of its complement: green over bright red, orange over blue, and yellow over purple. This method of graying wools often produces more unusual shades than dulling them with black. Khaki or Taupe dye will also tone down colors. Test a small sample before you dye a large piece.

To create a wonderful off-black for a background, collect a pile of dark colored scraps and overdye them with a dark dye or several dark colors, such as black, olive, and brown. The background will be interestingly varied, because of the hodgepodge of wools used. You can also use a lighter dye, such as Taupe or Bronze, over lighter colored wools to achieve a pleasing result.

Although dyeing with natural dyes is beyond the scope of this book, I would like to mention the use of onion skins to dye pastel wool. A pleasing golden brown dye is released when you gently simmer the dry outer skins of onions. You can place the skins in an old stocking for easy handling. The dye can then be used to give an interesting golden wash to pastel wools, uniting otherwise separate colors. For a spotted effect, onion skins can also be sandwiched between layers of pastel wool, salted, and simmered with enough water to prevent burning.

Spot-dyeing. Deliberately spotting crumpled wool with one or several dyes produces variegated pieces that can be used for special effects.

Spot-dyeing over pastels is another method for achieving an illusive coloring, particularly for backgrounds. Presoak the wool, usually a ¼-yard or a ½-yard piece, and, without wringing it out, crumple it in a flat pan. Spoon dissolved dye or dyes systematically over the top of your wool. Salt it, add only enough water to make it "swampy," and cover it loosely with foil. Simmer for about forty minutes, checking to be sure it doesn't boil dry. The resulting splotchy-looking piece will hook in beautifully! A very useful booklet that gives many interesting formulas for spot-dyeing is *Scraps and Spots* by Dotti Ebi (1979).

Preparing the Strips

Using Scissors

Once you have the fabric ready for your project, it is necessary to cut it into strips. The earliest rugs were made with fabric strips cut by hand with a pair of scissors, and this is still a perfectly acceptable way of working. In fact, purists deliberately use this method, feeling that the slight unevenness that occurs in hand cutting creates an antique appearance.

When cutting fabric into strips, it is advisable to tear your material into 1-inch or ½-inch strips, and then cut the strips with scissors. Using this method ensures against making off-grain, or bias, strips, which will pull apart when hooked. Some fabric, like tweeds or checks, may resist being torn. In this case, you must follow a thread as you cut. Any unevenness in the width of the strip is disguised when it is hooked, so use everything you cut.

The ideal length for wool strips is 12 to 18 inches.

Using Cutting Machines

Another method for cutting fabric strips is to use a cloth-cutting machine. Developed in the early twentieth cen-

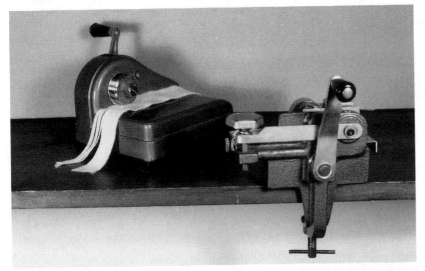

Hand-operated cutting machines, which make the preparation of wool strips easy, are available in two models.

tury, this small, hand-operated device cuts woolen fabric evenly and quickly, and most serious rug makers possess one. A cutting machine is designed to cut wool, and it doesn't easily accommodate other types of fabric.

There are two models: one that clamps to a table, and another that adheres to a flat surface with suction cups. Interchangeable cutter heads are available for making strips as narrow as $3/32$ inch and strips as wide as $1/4$ inch. When using the machine, it is advisable to tear your material into 3-inch strips, so that the torn edge acts as a guide for straight cutting.

The following guide will help you choose which cutter head to use:

#3 head cuts 6 strips $3/32$ inch wide
#4 head cuts 4 strips $1/8$ inch wide
#5 head cuts 3 strips $5/32$ inch wide
#6 head cuts 3 strips $3/16$ inch wide
#7 head cuts 2 strips $7/32$ inch wide
#8 head cuts 2 strips $1/4$ inch wide

It takes eight to nine hours to hook I square foot using #3 or #4 strips. It takes five to six hours to hook I square foot using #6 or #8 strips.

As with all machines, parts on a cutting machine may wear out. When cutter heads get dull, they can easily be replaced through the manufacturer. You can prolong the life of the cutter head if you try not to over-tighten the tension or cut a lot of fabric with a high proportion of synthetic fibers.

Choosing the Strip Width

The width of the strip you choose to use is determined by your own preference, as well as by the pattern you've selected. A bold, simple design can be rendered with wide strips (1/4-inch strips). When hooked in a manner that reinforces the design elements, wide strips add a secondary textural interest. When you are hooking with wide strips, the way the loops lie is very important, since your work will appear confused if the loops are at odds with the design.

If your pattern has a lot of detail or requires elaborate shading, a narrow strip (3/32 inch or 1/8 inch) is an appropriate choice. Narrow strips blend together easily, and the surface interest is more subtle.

Hooking Technique

Stretching the Backing

Although it is possible to hook while holding the back-ing in your hand, it is much easier to work on a tight backing. You can use a picture frame or a canvas stretcher

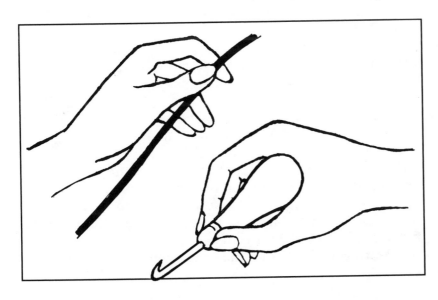

The hook may be held like a pencil, especially when working with fine strips.

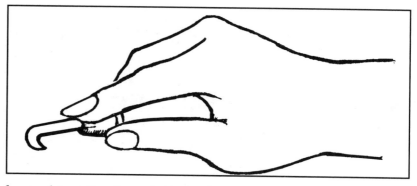

The hook may be "palmed" if that position is more comfortable or if you are working with wide strips.

by tacking the foundation, design side up, evenly to the frame and pulling it drum-tight. If you use a hoop, place the backing over the smaller ring, slide the larger ring over it, and tighten the thumb screw, pulling the backing taut as you tighten the hoop.

Holding the Hook

There are two ways to hold a rug hook. You can grasp it like a pencil with your thumb and forefinger on the metal collar. Or you can "palm" it, still keeping your thumb and forefinger on the collar, but placing the handle in your palm, so that it is covered by your whole hand. Your own comfort will dictate which method you should use.

Selecting a Work Area

You will need to select a comfortable and well-lighted area in which to work. Rest the frame or hoop in your lap or against a table as you sit comfortably in a chair or on a sofa. The frame should be tilted toward you, so that you are not leaning forward over it.

Tightening your hoop over hooked areas will not damage your work.

Starting to Hook

As you follow the directions given below, you will quickly master the technique of hooking.

1. With your left hand, hold the end of the wool strand between your thumb and forefinger.

2. Pick up the hook with your right hand. Place your fingertips on the metal collar to hold the hook like a pencil, or cover the handle with your hand.

3. With your left hand, hold the wool strip beneath and

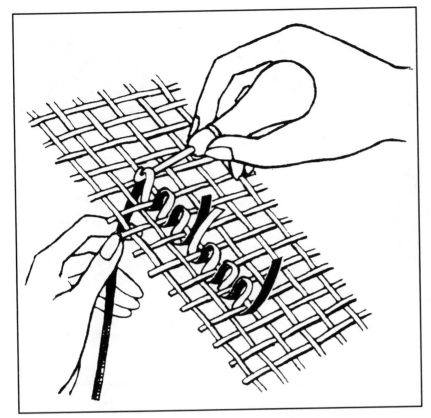

The strip of wool is held between the thumb and forefinger of the left hand, while the hook is held with the right hand. The hook is pushed through the backing and catches the wool strip. The shaft of the hook should touch your left forefinger; the barb of the hook should hit your thumb.

against the backing. With your right hand, push the hook through the mesh above your left hand. The shaft of the hook should touch your left forefinger, sliding behind the wool strip. The barb of the hook should hit your thumb, which pushes the wool onto the hook.

4. With the hook, pull the end of the strip through the weave, leaving a 1/2-inch tail.

5. Push the hook into the next weave, catching the wool and pulling it up to form a loop to a height equal to the width of the strip. *Note:* To prevent pulling the end of the strip out, lean the loop back toward the tail or the previous loop as you pull it up.

6. Working from right to left, make even loops that gently touch each other. *Note:* Whether you loop every weave or skip some depends on how tightly woven the backing is.

Hooking is not done in back-and-forth rows like needlepoint; areas are filled following their shapes, and hooking is done in the most convenient direction. Don't turn corners. Cut the strip and start again.

The tails at the beginnings and endings of strips are cut to the same height as the loops. They will not be noticeable between the loops.

7. When you reach the end of the strip, pull it to the surface.

8. Start a second strip in the same weave in which the previous strip ended, again leaving a ½-inch tail.

9. After making several loops with a new strip, trim the tails even with the loops.

Hooking in a Straight Line

Hooking from right to left, practice making even loops in a straight line following the weave of the backing. Try making a second row just above the first. Leave at least one thread between the rows; you may leave more, depending on the width of the strip and the weave of the backing.

If an area of hooking must have a straight edge, hook a row as a "fence." Then the row can easily be removed.

Hooking in Wavy Lines

When you are hooking confidently in straight lines, try working in wavy lines, making a curving line across the backing. Make a second row following the same curves. Then make two more wavy rows, working from *left to right*, to practice working in a different direction. Most people work comfortably in only a few directions, so they prefer to turn their work rather than to loop awkwardly.

The backs of hooked pieces should be covered with neat, even "stitches." Tails hanging down, crossovers, twisted rows, and large unfilled spaces are signs of poor technique.

Hooking in Circles

Practice working in circles. A circle should always be filled following the curve (unless the special requirements of the design dictate otherwise). First, hook the outline of the circle. Then fill the center by following the outline, turning your work as necessary to be comfortable.

Developing a Rhythm

To hook easily with a steady rhythm comes with practice. The synchronization of the hand movements may seem awkward at first, but as you become more proficient, the technique will become automatic. Then you will find hooking a relaxing and pleasurable pastime. Avoid hooking in uncomfortable directions, or your loops will become uneven and twisted. Cut the strip and begin again or turn your work.

To keep the tip of a leaf sharp, angle the cut end of the strip to form the narrow point.

Packing and Filling

As you hook, try to create a surface texture that is both attractive and durable. If too many loops are pulled into the backing, your work will tend to hump and will not lie flat. If the loops are too far apart, the backing will be visible, and your work will have a rough appearance. Both conditions can be corrected, the first by pulling out some loops to loosen the tension on the backing, and the second by adding more loops and rows.

Sawtoothing is a method of shading with narrow strips. Loops of one color are pulled up between those of another color. Usually the colors are close in value, but in the photo, the color contrast is exaggerated for clarity. Sawtoothing is usually used to shade an area sideways.

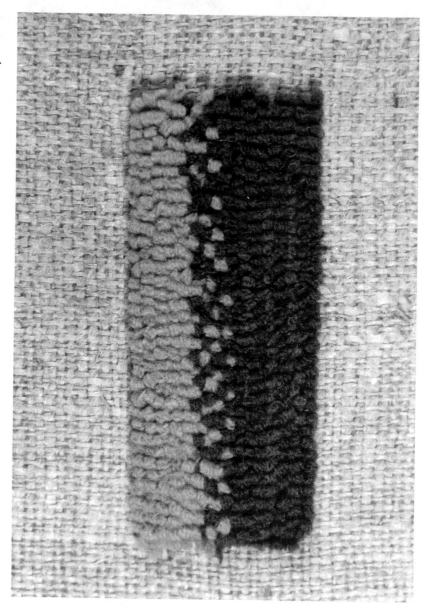

Pulling Out and Reusing Strips

Even the most experienced rugger must rework some areas, perhaps because a motif looks confused or the color doesn't work. It is usually easy to find an end of a strip and to pull it out. If the area is well packed, you may need to use tweezers. Strips can be reused if they are not too badly frayed.

Adjusting Your Technique to the Strip Width

I usually hold my hook like a pencil when I'm working with narrow #3 strips. The loops fall into place easily as I hook. When I hook with wider strips, such as #6 or #8, I "palm" the hook. By holding the hook at this more extreme angle, I find it easier to pick up the wide strip without twisting the loop. Twisted loops make your work appear confused.

Hooking Taboos

When you are hooking, avoid crossing a row of hooking with another strip. This will create lumps on the back of your work, so that the piece, especially a rug, will wear unevenly. The back of hooked pieces should be neat, covered with even, smooth stitches. If there are significant open spaces—1/8-inch to 1/4-inch spaces referred to as "holidays"—they should be filled in. If the rows of hooking appear ropelike on the back, you are twisting the strips (and using an excessive amount of wool). This is the result of looping the strip over the hook with your left hand. Turn your hook so that the barb will catch the strip. Any loose ends should be pulled to the surface and trimmed to a height even with the loops.

Shading

An astonishingly realistic effect can be achieved by shading, using close values of a color to create a three-dimensional appearance. Learning to shade takes practice, but it is not hard to do. Generally, the technique is used with narrow strips and involves sawtoothing or fingering.

Outlining is a way of separating areas that would otherwise be unclear.

Fingering is a method of shading in which the loops of one color are hooked between the rows of another color of close value. In the photo, the color contrast is exaggerated for clarity. Fingering is usually used to shade an area vertically.

Sawtoothing is a method in which loops of one color are hooked between loops of another, working rows in a zig-zag, or sawtoothed, fashion. You need to anticipate shading with a new color by leaving enough room between the loops to accommodate the new color. It may be necessary to hook several rows of sawtoothing to achieve a smooth transition.

A second method of shading is to finger a color between rows of another color. Again, the area to be shaded should not be worked too tightly, so that there will be room for additional loops.

A trick I sometimes use to create an even transition is what I call "cutting and scratching." Sometimes a minute dot of color is needed to achieve a perfect blending. I find that adding the loop or loops of the needed color, then clipping off the tops and scratching the area with the point of my scissors, often supplies the tiny bit of color needed.

Keeping the Work Area Neat

As you hook, little wool clippings tend to accumulate around you. You can keep a small container near at hand to put them in. Or you can vacuum your work with a Dust Buster—noisy but effective!

Maintenance of Hooked Pieces

Using Padding

Hooked rugs that are to be walked on should be protected with a nonskid padding. Synthetic pads are available where carpets are sold and are easily cut to size with scissors. Fiber pads are only appropriate for large, room-sized rugs, and they have the additional disadvantage of absorbing moisture over time. A stair runner should be professionally installed with appropriate padding placed under the tread sections.

The adhesive quality of synthetic padding is reduced when it gets dirty, but the padding can be hand washed to restore its grip. Keeping the padding clean will prolong its life, as well as that of your rugs.

Cleaning Rugs, Stair Runners, and Chair Seats

Soil is abrasive to any textile. Your hooked pieces, which represent hours of labor, deserve to be kept clean. Rugs should be vacuumed regularly, using a suction-type machine with gentle power. Occasionally, you should turn the rug over and pat it gently to dislodge grit that has fallen between the loops. Of course, you can't handle stair runners this way, so regular vacuuming is important. Chair seats don't usually need vacuuming, although it won't hurt them. If they are used a lot, they can be cleaned just like rugs.

Rugs that are walked on will eventually require cleaning. I recommend cleaning them at home unless you are sure a commercial cleaner will treat them gently. Harsh cleaners can damage textiles.

One of the better cleaning agents available is sodium lauryl sulphate. It is an extremely mild, highly concentrated synthetic detergent that is used by conservationists to clean textiles. It has a neutral pH, which means that it will not harm cellulose fibers (burlap, cotton, or linen) or protein fibers (wool). More important, it is free rinsing and will not leave a residue. I discovered this cleaner in a tack shop, where it is sold as Orvus WA Paste, displayed with horse shampoos and coat conditioners.

Ordinary household detergents have been recommended for cleaning hooked pieces, but they are generally highly alkaline, which makes them unsuitable for wool. They contain fillers and brighteners, which are damaging to textiles, and they leave a residue that attracts soil.

Procedure for Cleaning with Orvus

If possible, turn the hooked piece over and gently pat the back to remove any grit that might have lodged between the loops. Using a suction-type vacuum with gentle power, vacuum the surface of the rug. Dissolve 1 teaspoon of Orvus WA Paste in 1 quart of water. Dampen a clean sponge with this solution and gently rub a square-foot area at a time, wetting the surface of the piece without soaking it. Rinse the sponge, and wash off the Orvus with clear water. Allow the piece to dry flat in a shaded area.

Thoughtful care of your hooked pieces will keep them looking fresh and attractive, preserving them for future generations.

Beginner
Gift Projects

Rooster Brick Cover

This brick cover was inspired by one of our own primitive rug designs, which incorporated an old wooden weather vane with a hit-or-miss border. Ideal in an Early American setting, it can be used as a doorstop, a paperweight, or an attractive decorative piece. This photograph shows the brick cover hooked with #3 stripettes.

This brick cover is hooked with #6 stripettes. Notice the difference in texture compared with the version shown on page 49.

Rooster Brick Cover

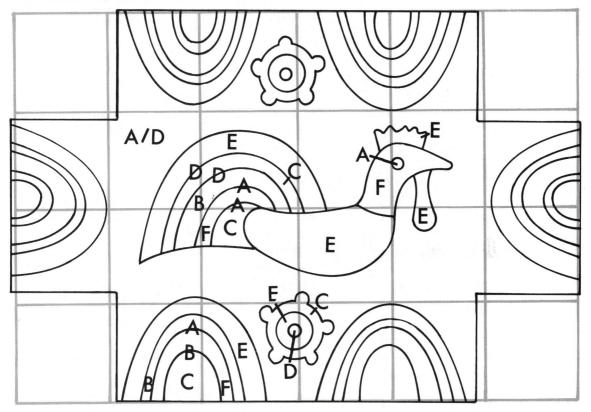

Model size: 8 inches by 4 inches by 2$\frac{1}{2}$ inches

Backing: 20-by-20-inch linen

Total wool amount: 4 ounces of #3 stripettes

　　　　　　　　　　　4$\frac{1}{2}$ ounces of #6 stripettes

Strip width: #3 ($\frac{3}{32}$ inch) and #6 ($\frac{3}{16}$ inch)

Color amounts needed for hooking:

		#3 stripettes	#6 stripettes
A.	Black #599	5	3
B.	Cinnamon #37/4	2	1
C.	Light blue #22/1	2	1
D.	Navy #6307	5	3
E.	Yellow, bright #35/5	3	2
F.	Yellow, pale #37/1	2	2

Enlarge by 200 percent to obtain 2-inch squares.

Colored swatches are identified by a number, such as #37/4, at the Dorr Mill Store. All Dorr swatches have six values of color. In this case, #37 refers to a cinnamon swatch, which varies from a pale yellow to a deep cinnamon. The 4 indicates the fourth value in the cinnamon gradation.

Materials needed for finishing:
   8-by-10-inch piece of fabric for bottom (corduroy, velveteen,
      or a pretty calico)
   Old pair of panty hose

Alternatives

This simple design will accommodate many color schemes, and it can be a scrap-user if you have bits and pieces of leftovers. However, using too many colors will result in a "clown's-pants" appearance.

Getting Started

Start hooking wherever you like, working *inside* the lines to prevent overfilling areas. Overfilling will distort the design, particularly when you are using #6 strips. Hook the eye of the rooster by making a dark circle and enlivening it with a loop of pale yellow in the center. Be sure to hook with the forms. Ragged edges indicate loops are not hooked closely enough. The navy and black are used as *one* background color to keep it interesting. After the hooking is completed, check the back for holidays.

Getting Finished

Check your work against the brick to be covered, and add or subtract rows, if necessary, to make it fit. Allow enough ease to put a little stuffing on top of the brick. Machine zigzag 1¼ inches beyond the hooking, and cut off the excess backing beyond the stitching. Using a steam iron or damp towel, press the brick cover on the right side. Using matching thread and working on the right side, pull the corners together and overcast the sides together. Stitch between the loops, so that the stitching is hidden.

To cover the rough surface of the brick, wrap it in the pants portion of an old pair of panty hose. To add roundness, mound one leg of the panty hose on top of the brick. (Cut off the other leg.) Slip the boxed top over this padding, and slip stitch a piece of fabric to the bottom, hiding your stitches between the hooked loops.

Chair Seat

The cornucopia motif on this chair seat is borrowed from the folk art tradition, but it is handled in a sophisticated way. The chair seat can be finished quickly to add a comfortable touch to a Boston rocker or Windsor chair. Hooked in a variety of colors, the pattern can be worked as a set for dining room chairs.

Chair Seat

Enlarge by 200 percent to
obtain 2-inch squares.

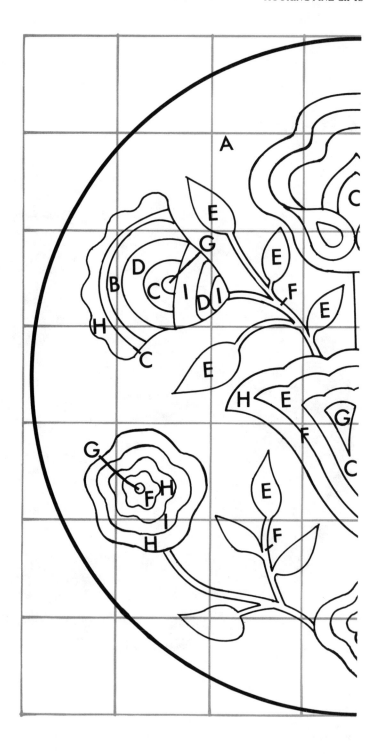

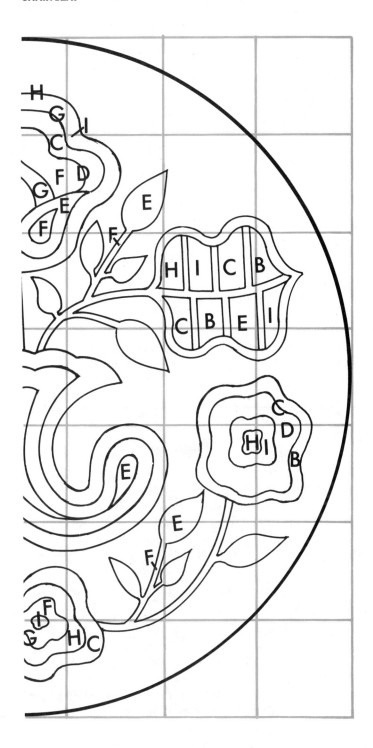

Model size: 14-inch round

Backing: 10-ounce burlap

Total wool amount: 8 ounces of scraps

Strip width: #6 (³/₁₆ inch)

Color amounts needed for hooking:

A.	Black-green	3	ounces
B.	Blue tweed	1	ounce
C.	Gold	¹/₂	ounce
D.	Gray-blue	¹/₂	ounce
E.	Light rust	1	ounce
F.	Peach	¹/₂	ounce
G.	Red-orange plaid	¹/₂	ounce
H.	White	¹/₂	ounce
I.	Yellow-green tweed	¹/₂	ounce

Material needed for finishing:

18-by-18-inch piece of matching or contrasting fabric for backing

Alternatives

There are many small areas to be filled in this design, so you can use up scraps with this project. I suggest making the leaves and stems a unifying element by keeping their colors the same or closely related. Too many colors can fragment a design. Consider your background color: you will want more vibrant colors if you're using a dark background, softer tones if your background is light.

Getting Started

It is easiest to hook from detail to surrounding area. Your hooking direction should follow the design. The pattern of the rows and loops should reinforce the shape of the motif. To maintain the circular shape of the chair seat, work two parallel rows of background around the edge. Then fill the remainder, following the shapes of the motifs. Check the finished piece for holidays.

Getting Finished

Machine zigzag one row of stitching 1 inch beyond the hooked edge, then cut the excess burlap. Turn under a hem and conceal it with a lining blind stitched to the edge. Press the chair seat on the right side, using a damp towel.

ROOSTER BRICK COVER
8 by 4 by 2¹/₂ inches.
#3 and #6 wool strips on linen.
Hooked by Happy DiFranza.

CHAIR SEAT
14-inch round.
#6 wool strips on burlap.
Hooked by Happy DiFranza.

NEW ENGLAND VILLAGE
11 by 14 inches.
#3 wool strips on linen.
Hooked by Happy DiFranza.

INITIAL PILLOW
14 by 14 inches.
#4 wool strips and 1/8-inch ribbon
on wool homespun.
Hooked by Happy DiFranza.

CHRISTMAS TOY ORNAMENTS
6 inches high.
#3 wool strips on burlap.
Hooked by Happy DiFranza.

RUSSIAN PILLOW
14 by 14 inches.
#3 wool strips on linen.
Hooked by Happy DiFranza.

CHINESE CLOUD FOOTSTOOL
12 by 17 inches.
#3 wool strips on linen.
Hooked by Happy DiFranza.

BAA BAA BLACK SHEEP RUG
22 by 30 inches.
#6 wool strips on linen.
Hooked by Elizabeth DiFranza.

PATCHWORK RUG
30 by 38 inches.
#8 wool strips on linen.
Hooked by Elizabeth DiFranza.

WELCOME RUG
37-by-18-inch half-round.
#6 wool strips on linen.
Hooked by Happy DiFranza.

BIRD-ON-THE-VINE RUG
20 by 30 inches.
#4 wool strips on linen.
Hooked by Suzanne Petretta.

WALL ANGEL
13 by 34 inches.
#6 wool strips on linen.
Hooked by Happy DiFranza.

FIREBOARD
28 by 28 inches.
#4 wool strips on linen.
Hooked by Happy DiFranza.

H&S

COME LIVE WITH ME

AND BE MY LOVE

AND WE WILL ALL THE

PLEASURES PROVE

NOVEMBER 14, 1959

WEDDING RUG
30 by 40 inches.
#4 wool strips on linen.
Hooked by Happy DiFranza.

STAIR RUNNER
Riser, 8½ by 28 inches;
Tread, 9½ by 28 inches.
#6 wool strips on linen.
Hooked by Suzanne Petretta.

TULIP BENCH COVER
18 by 36 inches.
#3 wool strips on linen.
Hooked by Happy DiFranza.

New England Village

Small pictures are always popular items. They can be finished very quickly, and they make wonderful gifts. Autumn is a favorite time of year in New England, and here is an opportunity to capture the bright colors of this season in a typical village scene.

New England Village

Enlarge by 200 percent to
obtain 2-inch squares.

Model size: 11 inches by 14 inches

Backing: 20-by-24-inch linen

Total wool amount: 6 ounces (30 #3 stripettes)

Strip width: #3 ($^3/_{32}$ inch)

Color amounts needed for hooking:

A.	Blue #15/1	4 stripettes
B.	Black #599	3 stripettes
C.	Bronze #32/2	1 stripette
D.	Brown #33/5	1 stripette
E.	Gold #30/5	2 stripettes
F.	Green #37/4	6 stripettes
G.	Green #28/5	1 stripette
H.	Peach #19/1	2 stripettes
I.	Red #7250	1 stripette
J.	Sand #37/2	4 stripettes
K.	Yellow #30/2	2 stripettes
L.	White #163	3 stripettes

2 yards black fingering yarn

1 yard black worsted yarn

2 yards white worsted yarn

Materials needed for finishing:

1 sheet of mat board

Spray Mount (available in art supply stores)

X-Acto knife

Double-stick carpet tape

$^5/_8$ yard fabric to cover mat

17-by-20-inch picture frame

Alternatives

There are several alternative ways to use this pattern. You may choose other colors to emphasize another season of the year. Because of the detail in this design, I suggest hooking areas of flat color. Or you can enlarge the pattern and add a border to make a rug.

Getting Started

Begin with any section you like, but always remember to hook details before working on the surrounding area. For example, hook the tree branches before adding the leaf area. Hook with the form of the design; the roofs, the sky, and the fields should be worked in horizontal rows. The details add charm to the scene, but they should not become oversized. Hook *inside* the lines. Be sure all the windows in a building are hooked with the same number of loops, so they will be uniform. When hooking is complete, check the back for holidays.

Using fingering yarn, add the black fences in the back, making a long stitch for the rail first and adding the pickets with short, parallel stitches. Using the heavier worsted, add the black fence by the church and the white fence around the common.

Getting Finished

Machine zigzag 1 inch beyond the hooking, and cut off the excess backing to the stitching. Using a steam iron or damp towel, press the picture on the right side.

Cut a piece of mat board 17 inches by 20 inches. To make a 3-inch mat, cut an opening 11 inches by 14 inches. Spray the back of the fabric with Spray Mount. Spray the fabric lightly without saturating it, and then allow it to become tacky. Center the mat board on the back of the fabric, smoothing the fabric against the mat board. Using an X-Acto knife, cut the fabric diagonally at each corner. Leaving a 1-inch border, cut away the fabric over the center opening. Fold the fabric borders so that they adhere to the back of the mat.

Cut another piece of mat board 17 inches by 20 inches. Place double-stick carpet tape in the center of the mat board, then press the picture down firmly on top of it. Place the fabric mat over the picture and center it in a frame.

Initial Pillow

A wedding gift that a bridal couple will love! This initial pillow is unusual and personal, and it can be completed easily and quickly. It is an especially versatile project: materials other than wool can be used, and the piece can be framed as a picture as well as finished as a pillow. You can choose to omit the initial and hook just the vines, or hook two pillows, one with an initial and vines, and one with vines only.

Model size: 14 inches by 14 inches
Backing: 20-by-22-inch wool homespun
Total wool amount: 2³/4 ounces of scraps
Total ribbon amount: Seven 10-yard rolls of ¹/8-inch ribbon
Strip and ribbon width: #4 (¹/8 inch)
Color amounts needed for hooking:

    Wool scraps

A.	Blue-gray	1¹/4	ounces
B.	Green tweed	1	ounce
C.	Green, dark	¹/2	ounce

    10-yard rolls of ¹/8-inch ribbon as follows:

D.	Blue	1
E.	Pink	1
F.	Red	1
G.	Rose	1
H.	Sapphire	1
I.	Yellow	2

Materials needed for finishing:

    ¹/2 yard of wool homespun or other backing fabric

    16-by-16-inch soft, muslin-covered pillow form

    2 yards of decorative braid

Alternatives

The initial should catch the viewer's attention, and a color of medium value works best. A light value will disappear against the background, and something very dark, like navy blue, will be too dominating. The vine and flowers must show clearly over the initial.

Enlarging and Transferring

Enlarge the initial and the vine to the desired size, and trace each part on separate pieces of pattern cloth, marking the corners of your pillow. Trace the initial onto the backing and mark the corners. (Adding margin lines will make the finishing difficult.) Matching corners, place the vine section over the initial, and trace the sections appropriate for your initial.

Initial Pillow

Enlarge by 200 percent to
obtain 2-inch squares.

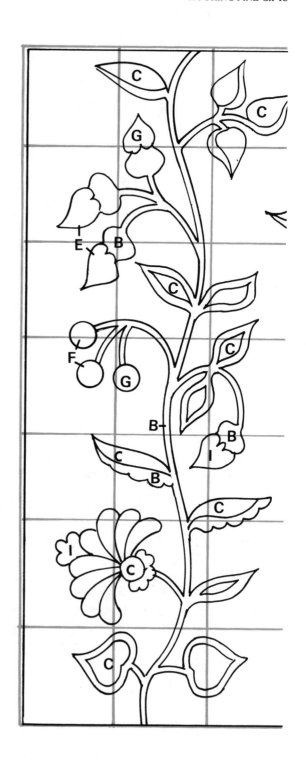

A B C D E F

G H I J K L

M N O P Q R

S T U V W X

Y Z

Lettering for Initial Pillow

Getting Started

Begin at any section, but always work the details before the surrounding areas. Hook the initial, following the shape of the letter. Loops on the edges of the motifs should be low and close to keep these edges sharp. When hooking with the ribbon, keep the loops close to form a dense and shiny texture that will contrast with the areas hooked with wool. After hooking is complete, check the back of your piece for holidays.

Getting Finished

Placing the front of your hooking against a folded Turkish towel, press it with a steam iron. Fold under the edges of your piece to make a square of the desired size and press the edges flat. Leaving 1/2 inch for a seam, cut off the excess backing. Place the right side of the hooked piece against the right side of your backing and machine stitch on three sides. Clip the corners, turn the pillow right side out, and insert the pillow form. Blind stitch the fourth side. Sew decorative braid around the edge by hand.

Christmas Toy Ornaments

When this project is completed, a Santa, a train, and a toy soldier can dance around your Christmas tree. Quickly finished and assembled, these Christmas ornaments make perfect gifts for a favorite child or for older friends who are young at heart.

Model sizes: Approximately 6 inches high

Backing: 20-by-20-inch, 13-ounce burlap for three projects

Total wool amount: 2½ ounces of #3 stripettes for three projects

Strip width: #3 (³/₃₂ inch)

Color amounts needed for hooking three projects:

A.	Black #599	1 stripette
B.	Blue #15/6	2 stripettes
C.	Flesh #20/1	1 stripette
D.	Gold #31/3	2 stripettes
E.	Red #7250	2 stripettes
F.	White #163	2 stripettes
G.	Yellow-green #27/3	1 stripette
	Gold cloisonné thread	10 yards

Materials needed for finishing:

Light cardboard for backing

12-by-12-inch piece of felt for backing three projects

Elmer's Glue-All

X-Acto knife or scissors

Alternatives

Since these are holiday decorations, tradition demands gay colors. There are not many alternatives to the red, white, and black combination for Santa, although the boots and belt could be dark brown, and the red could be more orange or purple. The edge section, if not gold, should define the Santa and not blend with his white beard or red suit. A greater variety of colors can be used for the train and soldier, but keep them bright and distinct, so that the parts of each design are clear when viewed at a distance.

Materials other than wool fabric can also be used. Santa's beard and the white fur on his hat and coat can be worked with fuzzy yarn or French knots. Ribbon can also be used. (See directions for making the Initial Pillow.)

Getting Started

Start at any section, but work the details before the surrounding areas of color. Keep the loops low, even, and close, so that the areas of color will be clear. Uneven edges

Christmas Toy Ornaments

Enlarge by 200 percent to
obtain 2-inch squares.

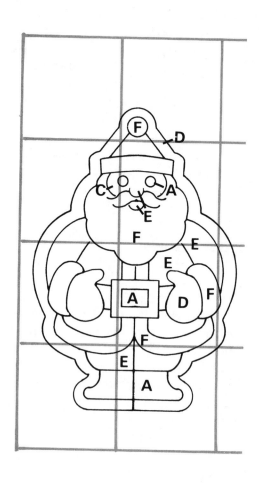

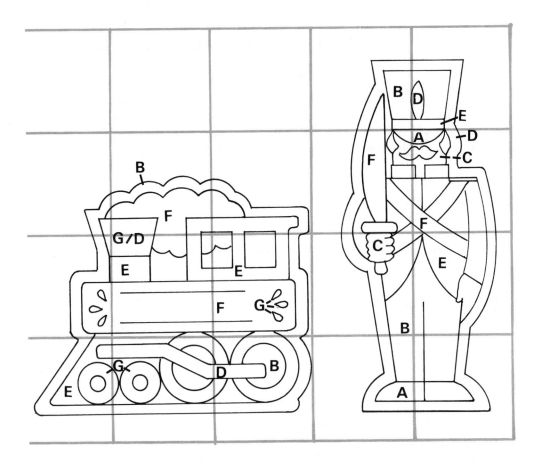

indicate that the loops are not worked closely enough. Add the gold cloisonné thread *after* you have completed hooking the project. Check all the pieces for holidays.

Getting Finished

Press your work on the right side with a steam iron or over a damp towel. Outline each ornament with a 1/4-inch row of Elmer's Glue-All, pushing it up against the last row of hooking so that the edge is well coated. When the glue is dry and transparent, cut out the ornament at the last hooked row; there will be no backing edge left. Glue your ornament to cardboard and, using an X-Acto knife, cut away the excess cardboard. Add a loop of gold thread at the top for a hanger. Glue felt over the cardboard. Run more glue around the edge of the ornament, and apply two rows of cloissoné thread to decorate the edge.

Intermediate and Advanced Gift Projects

Russian Pillow

With former Communist countries opening up to the West, new and exciting decorative ideas are influencing American designers. This pillow, adapted from Russian folk art, will add warmth and color to any interior.

Russian Pillow

Enlarge by 200 percent to
obtain 2-inch squares.

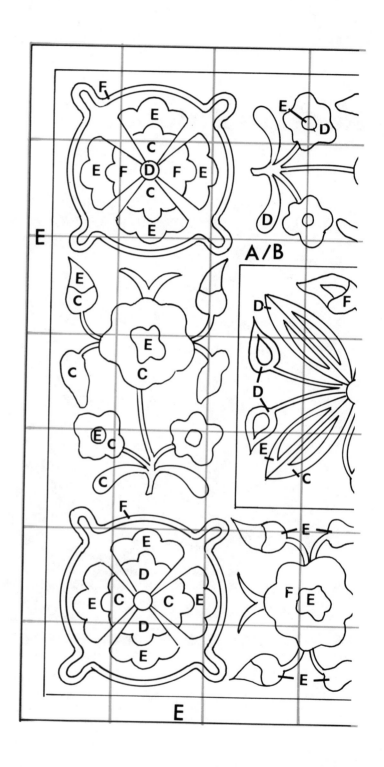

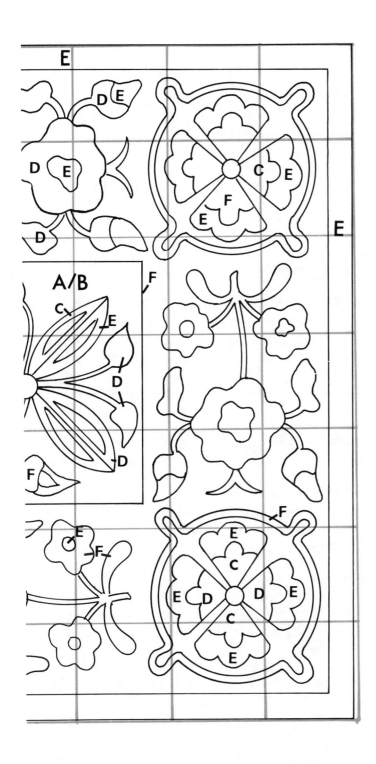

Model size: 14 inches by 14 inches
Backing: 20-by-25-inch linen
Total wool amount: 7 ounces of scraps, dyed wool, and #3 stripettes
Strip width: #3 (³/₃₂ inch)
Color amounts needed for hooking:

    A. Black #599   2 ounces (10 stripettes)
    B. Black-red #5/6   2 ounces (10 stripettes)
    C. Blue   4 stripettes
    D. Cream #100   2 stripettes
    E. Rose-pink   1 ounce of dyed wool (five 3-by-12-inch pieces)
    F. Yellow #30/4   3 stripettes

Materials needed for finishing:

    ¹/₂ yard fabric for backing pillow
    16-by-16-inch soft, muslin-covered pillow form
    2 yards of decorative braid

Directions for Dyeing Rose-Pink (TOD #31/101)

You will need one package each of Cardinal, Mahogany, and Maroon Cushing Perfection Dyes.

TOD #31/101. Dissolve ¹/₂ teaspoon Cardinal, ¹/₁₆ teaspoon Maroon, and ¹/₁₆ teaspoon Mahogany in 1 cup boiling water. Use ¹/₈ teaspoon of formula for each 3-by-12-inch white piece.

Alternatives

Since the design for this pillow was adapted from a Ukrainian embroidery, we selected lively colors to reflect the spirit of the original, but many different combinations can be used. To prevent confusion with a design composed of so many small motifs, you should limit the number of colors you choose.

Getting Started

Begin at any section, always working the details before the surrounding areas. Follow the forms of the designs when filling the shapes, and add the background in the same manner, picking up the graceful curves of the motifs. Be sure single rows of a color do not disappear; it may be necessary to adjust them after the background is added. Hook the edge with five parallel rows of hooking. Check your piece for holidays.

TOD refers to a formula number in Book I from The Triple Over Dye Family. (See Sources of Supply.)

Getting Finished

Machine zigzag 1 inch from the last row of hooking. Cut off the excess burlap beyond the stitching. Using a damp towel, press the piece on the right side. With right sides together, stitch the pillow backing and the hooked piece together on three sides. Insert the pillow form, and blind stitch the fourth side. By hand, add decorative braid around the edge to hide the seam.

Chinese Cloud Footstool

Rest your tired feet on this Chinese "floating cloud." Our model was sized to a footstool obtained through the Bombay Company. You may find a footstool in an antiques
shop or in your attic at home. The pattern can be easily adjusted to various sizes by
adding or subtracting lines of hooking to accommodate your special piece.

Model size: 12 inches by 17 inches for footstool with slip seat

Backing: 20-by-25-inch linen

Total wool amount: 8 ounces of wool or 39 stripettes

Strip width: #3 (³/₃₂ inch)

Color amounts needed for hooking:

A.	Cream #100	4 stripettes
B.	Maroon #20/5	4 stripettes
C.	Pink, light #20/1	6 stripettes
D.	Pink, medium #20/2	3 stripettes
E.	Pink, dark #20/3	8 stripettes
F.	Tan #37/2	2 stripettes
G.	Turquoise, light #26/2	3 stripettes
H.	Turquoise, medium #26/4	3 stripettes
I.	Turquoise, dark #26/6	3 stripettes
J.	Yellow #37/1	3 stripettes

Materials needed for finishing:

Staple gun

Alternatives

Any number of color combinations can be used for this design, but be careful not to use too many colors. Only four colors were used for the model, with different values of the colors playing a double role as a separate color and as a related color that unifies the design. Of course, tweeds could be used very effectively in a design like this, and segments can be outlined, as well. Be sure each stripe is distinct, but don't let one stripe dominate the entire footstool design.

Getting Started

Check the size of your footstool, and adjust the design as necessary. Start at any section. The rows of hooking should follow the direction of each stripe, so that the pattern of rows reinforces the design concept. After you have finished hooking the project, check the back of the piece for holidays.

Getting Finished

Measure your hooked piece against the top of the footstool to be upholstered, and add or subtract rows of hook-

Chinese Cloud Footstool

Enlarge by 200 percent to
obtain 2-inch squares.

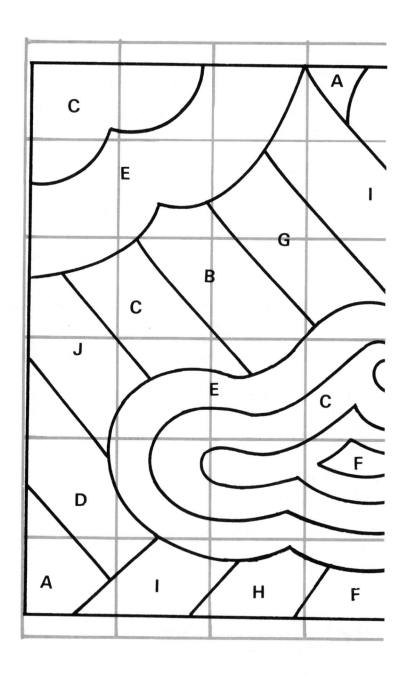

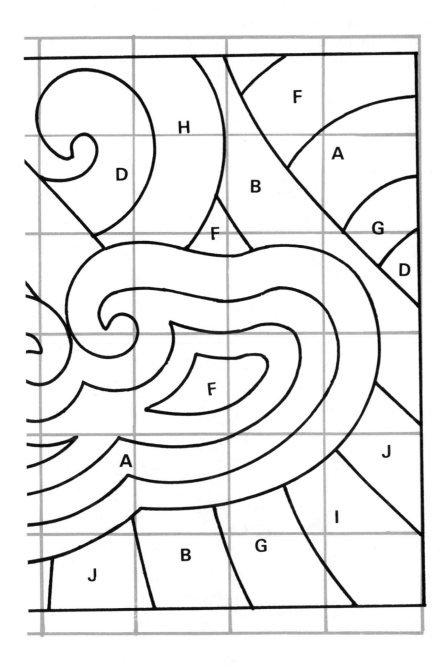

ing if necessary. (Patterns shrink slightly as they are hooked.) Check the back for holidays, and then press the piece on the right side with a damp towel. Leave enough backing to pull around the padded top, and staple or tack it to the underside.

Baa Baa Black Sheep Rug

The very first rug we designed was a children's rug for our firstborn, Elizabeth. When we decided to include this whimsical project in this book, Elizabeth volunteered to hook the rug for us. It can be put on the floor or used as a wall decoration. Either way, it will become a treasured piece, passed on from generation to generation.

Baa Baa Black Sheep Rug

Enlarge by 400 percent to
obtain 2-inch squares.

Model size: 22 inches by 30 inches
Backing: 30-by-48-inch linen
Total wool amount: 2 1/2 pounds of scraps
Strip width: #6 (3/16 inch)
Color amounts needed for hooking:

A.	Black	8 ounces
B.	Blue	3 ounces
C.	Gray-brown	3 ounces
D.	Gray, light	I ounce
E.	Pink, light	2 ounces
F.	Pink, medium	3 ounces
G.	White, assorted shades	14 ounces
H.	Yellow, bright	I ounce
I.	Yellow, medium	2 ounces
J.	Yellow-green	4 ounces

Materials needed for finishing:

3 1/2 yards of 1 1/4-inch twill tape

3 1/2 yards of #200 cording and 52 yards of triple-strand Persian yarn for whipping edge (optional)

Alternatives

Since this design was created for the young at heart, the colors should be bright. One sheep could be colored rather than white. Of course, the outlining can be a color other than black, or it can be omitted.

Getting Started

Before starting to hook, decide whether you wish to finish your project with twill tape or with a whipped edge. (See Getting Finished.) Start at any section. If you are outlining the forms, hook the outlining first and then fill. The sheep should be hooked following the undulating outline, so that a subtle, wavy pattern is created. The background bands should be hooked in undulating, parallel rows. Work the lettering carefully, keeping the loops close, so that the edges are clear and sharp. Hook *inside* the lines so that the letters do not become oversized, and adjust the rows if necessary. When the hooking is completed, check the back of your piece for holidays.

Getting Finished

To finish a rug with twill tape, select twill tape to match the edge of your rug and machine stitch it around the edge *before* starting to hook. Machine zigzag two rows 1 inch beyond the pattern margin. As you hook the rug, work right up to the tape. After completing the rug, cut off the excess burlap at the double line of zigzag stitching. Hem the tape over the backing edge. Using a damp towel, press your rug on the right side.

To finish a rug with a whipped edge, machine zigzag 1¼ inches beyond the last row of hooking and cut off the excess backing. Slip a piece of cording under the edge of the excess backing, pushing it right up against your last hooked row. Baste if you wish. Whipstitch this ridge. Using a tapestry needle threaded with a triple strand of Persian yarn, hide the knot in the cording. Bring the needle through to the front at the edge of the last row of hooking. Insert the needle from the back to the front again, bringing it through right next to the last stitch. Continue in this manner, completely covering the corded backing. Blind stitch twill tape over the narrow, exposed backing edge. Using a damp towel, press your piece on the right side.

Patchwork Rug

Quilting designs have often inspired rug designs, and this patchwork rug is a good example. You can use scraps that have accumulated from other projects, or you can collect fabric especially for this rug.

Model size: 30 inches by 38 inches
Backing: 37-by-48-inch linen
Total wool amount: 40 ounces of scraps
Strip width: #8 ($1/4$ inch)
Color amounts needed for hooking:

A.	Black	8 ounces
B.	Blue, light	2 ounces
C.	Blue, medium	7 ounces
D.	Brown-rust	3 ounces
E.	Gray, light	I ounce
F.	Gray, dark	2 ounces
G.	Green	I ounce
H.	Pink	I ounce
I.	Plum	2 ounces
J.	Rust, light	I ounce
K.	Rust, bright	8 ounces
L.	Sapphire	2 ounces
M.	Tan	2 ounces

Materials needed for finishing:

4 yards of $1 1/4$-inch twill tape
4 yards of #200 cording (optional)
70 yards of triple-strand Persian yarn (optional)

Alternatives

This kind of pattern will accommodate a variety of scraps. However, to use bits and pieces effectively, they must be organized. If you analyze the colors broadly in the model, you will see that there are only four main hues; the other colors can be considered shades or variants of the principal colors. Therefore, if you wish to change the color scheme, start by choosing four principal hues, sorting your scraps into four piles. Then find scraps that are related to these main colors. Using this system, you can probably come up with eight or nine additional shades. These will add excitement to your piece without creating a confusion of colors.

Getting Started

Before starting to hook, decide whether you wish to finish your project with twill tape or with a whipped edge.

Patchwork Rug

Enlarge by 400 percent to
obtain 2-inch squares.

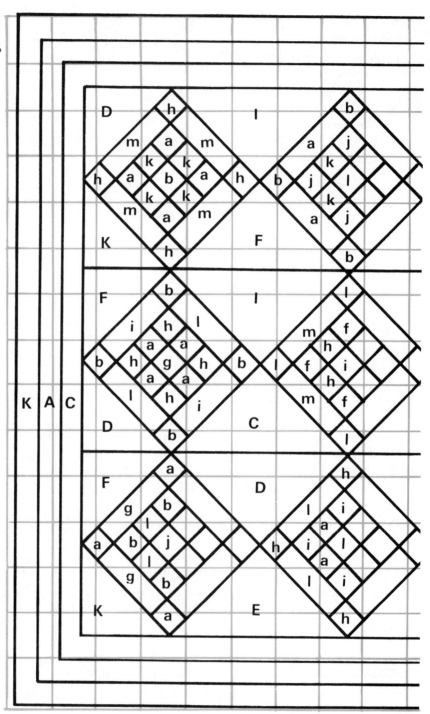

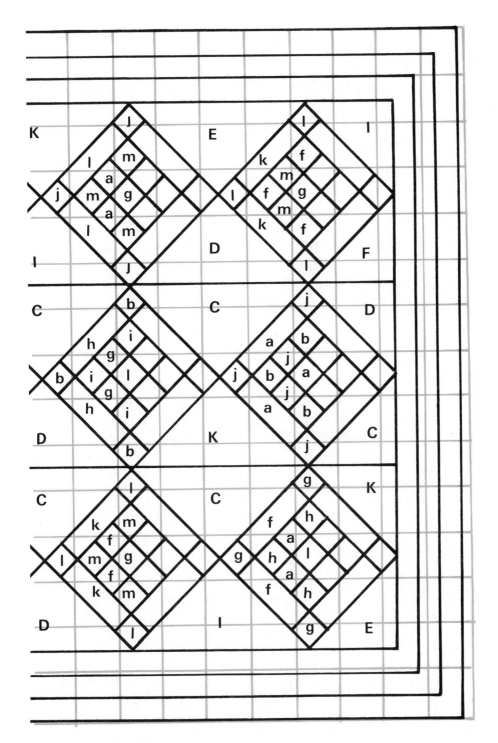

Both methods are described under Getting Finished. Start with any section. Parallel hooking is appropriate for this kind of design; all the sections were worked this way. The borders should be hooked in parallel rows. After hooking is completed, check the back of your piece for holidays.

Getting Finished

To finish a rug with twill tape, select twill tape to match the edge of your rug, and machine stitch it around the edge *before* starting to hook. Machine zigzag two rows 1 inch beyond the pattern margin. As you hook the rug, work right up to the tape. After completing the rug, cut off the excess burlap at the double line of zigzag stitching. Hem the tape over the backing edge. Using a damp towel, press your rug on the right side.

To finish a rug with a whipped edge, machine zigzag 1¼ inches beyond the last row of hooking and cut off the excess backing. Slip a piece of cording under the edge of the excess backing, pushing it right up against your last hooked row. Baste if you wish. Whipstitch this ridge. Using a tapestry needle threaded with a triple strand of Persian yarn, hide the knot in the cording. Bring the needle through to the front at the edge of the last row of hooking. Insert the needle from the back to the front again, bringing it through right next to the last stitch. Continue in this manner, completely covering the corded backing. Blind stitch twill tape over the narrow, exposed backing edge. Using a damp towel, press your piece on the right side.

Welcome Rug

This traditional half-round offers a welcome to all who enter. The Shaker Tree of Comfort adds a soothing elegance to any doorway.

Welcome Rug

Enlarge by 400 percent to
obtain 2-inch squares.

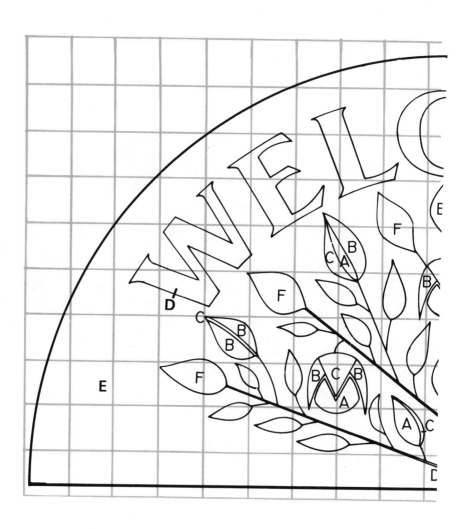

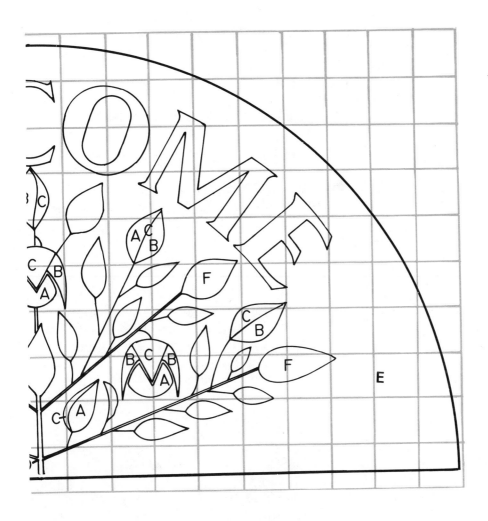

Model size: 37 inches by 18 inches, half-round
Backing: 28-by-48-inch linen
Total wool amount: 26 ounces of scraps and dyed wool
Strip width: #6 ($^3/_{16}$ inch)
Color amounts needed for hooking:

A.	Blue check	1 ounce
B.	Blue, light	1 ounce
C.	Blue, dark	1 ounce
D.	Gold	4 ounces ($^1/_3$ yard) of dyed wool
E.	Wine	1$^1/_4$ pounds
F.	Yellow-green and gold	2 ounces

Materials needed for finishing:

3 yards of 1$^1/_4$-inch twill tape
3 yards of #200 cording (optional)
54 yards of triple-strand Persian yarn (optional)

Directions for Dyeing Gold

You will need one package of Old Gold Cushing Perfection Dye. Dye $^1/_3$ yard of white material with $^9/_{32}$ teaspoon of dry Old Gold.

Alternatives

If the rug is to be used at the entrance of a home, use a dark, practical background. Keep the motifs strongly colored to be readable. If the rug is to be used inside your home (at the entrance to a guest room, for instance), you can choose lighter colors. The simplicity of the design lends itself to using simple, flat color areas, but the colors must be carefully balanced so that the design works as a whole.

Getting Started

Before starting to hook, decide whether you wish to finish your project with twill tape or with a whipped edge. Both methods are described under Getting Finished. Start at any section. Insert your initials and the date in the lower corners if you like. Hook the motifs of the design first. Then hook the background following the curves of the leaves and flowers. As you hook the lettering, work *inside* the lines, so the letters do not become oversized. The loops must be even and close to keep the edges clear and sharp. If the shape of the rug has been distorted, add or subtract rows of hooking to straighten the edge. After the hooking is completed, check the back of your rug for holidays.

Getting Finished

To finish your rug with twill tape, select 1¼-inch twill tape to match the edge of your rug, and machine stitch it around the edge *before* starting to hook. Machine zigzag two rows 1 inch beyond the pattern margin. As you hook the rug, work right up to the tape. After completing the rug, cut off the excess burlap beyond the zigzag stitching. Hem the tape over the backing edge. Using a damp towel, press your rug on the right side.

To finish your rug with a whipped edge, machine zigzag 1¼ inches beyond the last row of hooking and cut off the excess backing. Slip a piece of cording under the edge of the excess backing, pushing it right up against your last hooked row. Baste if you wish. Whipstitch this ridge. Using a tapestry needle threaded with a triple strand of Persian yarn, hide the knot in the cording. Bring the needle through to the front at the edge of the last row of hooking. Insert the needle from the back to the front again, bringing it through right next to the last stitch. Continue in this manner, completely covering the corded backing. Blind stitch twill tape over the narrow, exposed backing edge. Using a damp towel, press your piece on the right side.

Bird-on-the-Vine Rug

Grape and strawberry vines entwine to form an enchanting border around a colorful fantasy bird. The delicacy of the design makes this rug a charming addition to a lady's room.

Model size: 20 inches by 30 inches
Backing: 28-by-37-inch linen
Total wool amount: 29 ounces of scraps and dyed wool
Strip width: #4 ($^1/_8$ inch)
Color amounts needed for hooking:

A.	Black	I strip for bird's eye
B.	Blue	2 ounces scraps
C.	Brown	2 ounces of dyed wool
D.	Cream	16 ounces of dyed wool (I$^1/_3$ yards)
E.	Gold	3-by-12 inch piece
F.	Green, light	2 ounces of dyed wool
G.	Green, dark	3 ounces of dyed wool
H.	Green tweed	I ounce scraps
I.	Lavender	2 ounces scraps
J.	Red	I ounce scraps

Materials needed for finishing:

3 yards of I$^1/_4$-inch twill tape
3 yards of #100 cording (optional)
35 yards of triple-strand Persian yarn (optional)

Directions for Dyeing Cream, Light and Dark Green, and Brown

You will need one package each of Bronze Green, Golden Brown, and Old Ivory Cushing Perfection Dyes.

Cream. Using four $^1/_3$-yard pieces, dye each piece with $^1/_4$ teaspoon of dry Old Ivory. If there is some variation in the color of the dyed pieces, the slightly different shades will add life to your background.

Light and Dark Green. Dissolve $^1/_2$ teaspoon of Bronze Green dye in 1 cup of boiling water. Using 6-by-12-inch white pieces, dye six pieces with 1 teaspoon of the solution and seven pieces with 3 teaspoons for two different values of the same color.

Brown. Dissolve $^1/_2$ teaspoon of Golden Brown in 1 cup of boiling water. Using four 6-by-12-inch pieces of white wool, dye each piece with 5 teaspoons of dissolved dye.

Alternatives

This rug could be hooked with a dark background or a light one. If you choose a dark background, be sure the

Bird-on-the-Vine Rug

Enlarge by 400 percent to
obtain 2-inch squares.

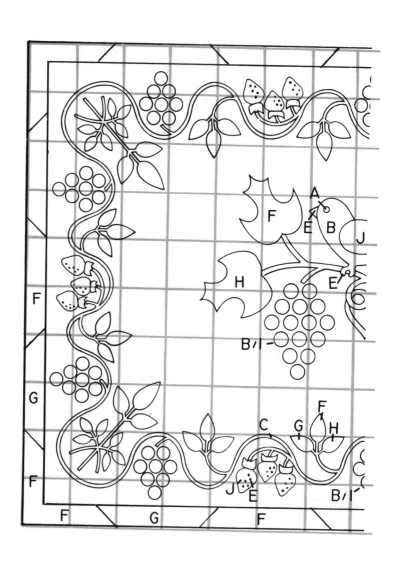

colors of the motifs are light and vibrant enough to be distinct. This kind of design can be a scrap-user, since the strawberries and grapes don't need to be exactly the same. The leaves of the vine may be different, too. A certain amount of variation will add charm to your work.

Getting Started

Before starting to hook, decide whether you wish to finish your project with twill tape or with a whipped edge. Both methods are described under Getting Finished. Begin with any section. Although it is customary to hook the details before doing the surrounding area, it is easier to squeeze in the bird's eye after the head is hooked. You can also add the strawberry seeds after hooking the berries. When working the background, follow the curves of the design. Hook the border in parallel rows. When the hooking is completed, check the back of your piece for holidays.

Getting Finished

To finish your rug with twill tape, select 1¼-inch twill tape to match the edge of your rug, and machine stitch it around the edge *before* starting to hook. Machine zigzag two rows 1 inch beyond the pattern margin. As you hook the rug, work right up to the tape. After completing the rug, cut off the excess burlap beyond the zigzag stitching. Hem the tape over the backing edge. Using a damp towel, press your rug on the right side.

To finish your rug with a whipped edge, machine zigzag 1¼ inches beyond the last row of hooking and cut off the excess backing. Slip a piece of cording under the edge of the excess backing, pushing it right up against your last hooked row. Baste if you wish. Whipstitch this ridge. Using a tapestry needle threaded with a triple strand of Persian yarn, hide the knot in the cording. Bring the needle through to the front at the edge of the last row of hooking. Insert the needle from the back to the front again, bringing it through right next to the last stitch. Continue in this manner, completely covering the corded backing. Blind stitch twill tape over the narrow, exposed backing edge. Using a damp towel, press your piece on the right side.

Wall Angel

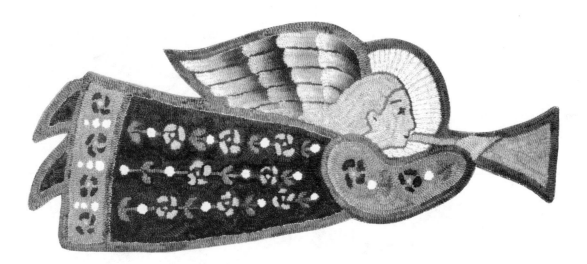

This wall angel, which was inspired by those wonderful Bavarian Christmas cookies, will add a festive note to any room. You can use a variety of materials with this project and let fancy be your guide.

Wall Angel

Enlarge by 400 percent to
obtain 2-inch squares.

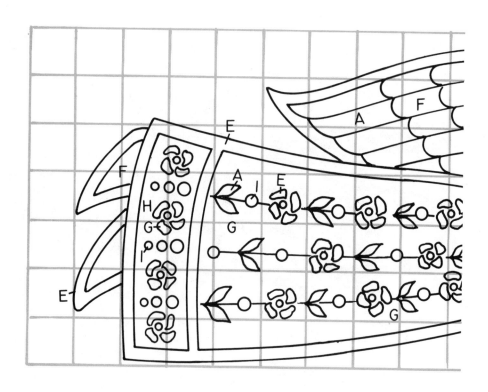

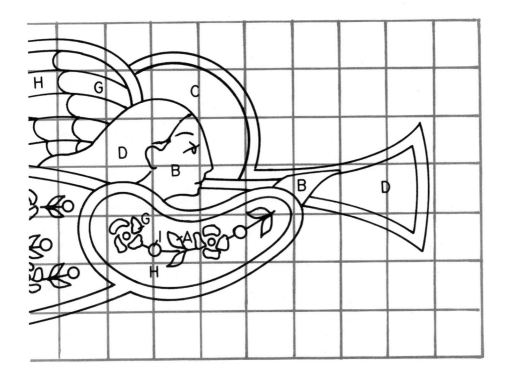

Model size: 13 inches by 34 inches

Backing: 22-by-48-inch linen

Total wool amount: 1¼ pounds of scraps and dyed wool

Strip width: #6 (³/₁₆ inch)

Color amounts needed for hooking:

Scraps and dyed wool:

A.	Blue-green	3-by-18-inch piece
B.	Flesh	6-by-12-inch scrap
C.	Gold, light	½ ounce dyed wool
D.	Gold, medium	1 ounce dyed wool
E.	Gold, dark	½ ounce dyed wool
F.	Purple	3-by-18-inch piece
G.	Red	3 ounces dyed wool
H.	Rose	4 ounces dyed wool
I.	White	3-by-18-inch piece
J.	Gold cloisonné thread	34 yards

Dip-dyed pieces:

Blue-green to white	three 3-by-18-inch pieces
Purple to white	three 3-by-18-inch pieces
Red to white	two 3-by-18-inch pieces
Rose to white	two 3-by-18-inch pieces

Materials needed for finishing:

3½ yards decorative gold braid for edging

Common pins

Gator board for mounting (available at art supply stores)

Colored marker to match edge

Mat knife or X-Acto knife

Elmer's Glue-All

Double-stick cloth carpet tape

Emery board or fine sandpaper

Adhesive hangers

Fish line for hanging

Directions for Dyeing the Colors

You will need one package each of Blue, Bright Purple, Buttercup, Cardinal, Cherry, Old Gold, Mahogany, Maroon, Reseda, and Yellow Cushing Perfection Dyes. Dissolve the dye amounts given in each formula in 1 cup of boiling water. Measure specific amounts from each cup. Use white wool pieces 3 inches by 18 inches.

TOD #31/101 (Rose-Red). Use $1/2$ teaspoon Cardinal, $1/16$ teaspoon Maroon, and $1/16$ teaspoon Mahogany.

Green Mountain Colors #2 (Gold). Use $1/32$ teaspoon Yellow, $4/32$ teaspoon Old Gold, and $1/32$ teaspoon Buttercup.

Green Mountain Colors #14 (Blue-Green). Use $1/32$ teaspoon Old Gold, $4/32$ teaspoon Blue, and $1/32$ teaspoon Reseda.

Green Mountain Colors #20 (Purple). Use $1/32$ teaspoon Cherry, $1/32$ teaspoon Blue, and $1/4$ teaspoon Bright Purple.

Use the following formulas to dye the colors for the angel's dress and feathers.

TOD #31/101 (Rose-Red). Dye four pieces with $1/2$ teaspoon dye for the sleeve and hem.

Dye ten pieces with 1 tablespoon dye for the dress.

Dip-dye two pieces with $1/2$ teaspoon dye for the rose-colored feathers.

Dip-dye two pieces with 1 tablespoon dye for the deeper red feathers.

Use the following formulas to dye the colors for the angel's hair, halo, and trumpet and for the outline around the angel.

Green Mountain Colors #2 (Gold). Dye two pieces with $1/2$ teaspoon dye for the halo.

Dye four pieces with 1 tablespoon dye for the hair and the trumpet.

Dye eight pieces with 3 tablespoons dye for the outline.

Use the following formulas to dye the colors for the leaves and feathers.

Green Mountain Colors #14 (Blue-Green). Dye two pieces with 2 teaspoons dye for the leaves.

Dip-dye three pieces with 2 tablespoons dye for the feathers of the angel.

Use the following formulas to dye the colors for the feathers and shoes.

Green Mountain Colors #20 (Purple). Dye one piece with 1 tablespoon dye for the shoes.

Dip-dye three pieces with 2 tablespoons dye for the feathers of the angel.

Alternatives

The most obvious way to vary the colors in this design is to change the colors of the dress, shoes, and wings. The new colors must relate to the others, however, so that the design does not become fragmented.

Getting Started

You can start with any section. Hook the details before doing the surrounding areas. For example, hook a flower on the dress and then add the background around it. When working the face, be sure the features do not become oversized. Don't hesitate to push the loops around with your hook, so that they lie correctly to give the impression you want.

When hooking with dip-dyed pieces, work in the most comfortable direction, starting at the light end or at the dark end of the feather and using the corresponding end of your strip. The feather should automatically shade into dark, medium, and light sections of color. Since the feather sections are of different sizes, only portions of the strip will be used in some cases. Pull the loops high to bring up the color section you need, and cut them. Save the leftovers to fill in another area.

Add the cloisonné thread last, squeezing it between the rows of hooking to edge the sections of the dress, the inside portion of the trumpet, the outside of the wing section, and the tips of the wings. To enliven the halo, fan long stitches at even intervals between the face and the edging.

After hooking, check your work for holidays.

Getting Finished

Press the angel on the right side with a damp towel. Place the angel on brown paper or newspaper. Using

Elmer's Glue-All, apply a ¼-inch line of glue all around the edge, pushing it up against the loops of the last row of hooking and rubbing it into the backing. Allow the glue to dry thoroughly—until the glue appears clear and the edge is "plasticized." Using an X-Acto knife or mat knife, cut around the angel close to the hooking to remove the excess backing. Apply double-stick carpet tape to the gator board, and place your angel on top, pressing it in place to make sure it adheres well. Cut around the angel with the knife. Smooth the edge with fine sandpaper. Color the edge with a marker matching the edge of the angel. Using Elmer's Glue, apply gold braid around the edge, holding it in place with common pins. Apply adhesive hangers to the back. Since this is a seasonal piece that will not be hung permanently, suspend it with fish line from small nails placed at the juncture of the wall and ceiling.

Fireboard

This fireboard, adapted from the art-deco era, has wonderful muted tones that fit beautifully into a formal setting.

Model size: 28 inches by 28 inches

Backing: 36-by-38-inch linen

Total wool amount: 3½ pounds of dyed wool and scraps

Strip width: #4 (⅛ inch)

Color amounts needed for hooking:

- A. Blue dip-dyed with Rust — four 3-by-12-inch wool pieces
- B. Bright gold — ½ yard
- C. Coral — two 6-by-12-inch scraps
- D. Dark brown — ⅓ yard of dyed wool
- E. Orange — 3-by-12-inch scrap
- F. Red-orange — 3-by-12-inch scrap
- G. Rust-brown — 3½ yards of dyed wool

Materials needed for finishing:

½-inch plywood sheet large enough to cover the fireplace opening and
  to make back supports

Four 3-inch hinges

½-inch molding to go around the complete fireboard

Wood stain

Double-stick carpet tape

Stapler or tacks

Elmer's Glue-All

Directions for Dyeing the Colors

You will need one package each of Aqualon Yellow, Dark Brown, Mahogany, and Mummy Cushing Perfection Dyes.

Blue Dip-Dyed with Rust. Dip-dye four 3-by-12-inch light blue pieces with 2 tablespoons Mummy from a solution of ¼ teaspoon Mummy dissolved in ½ cup boiling water.

Bright Gold. Dye ½ yard of white or off-white wool with ½ teaspoon of dry Aqualon Yellow.

Dark Brown and Rust-Brown. Dye four ½-yard pieces of white or off-white wool with ¼ teaspoon of dry Mummy for each piece to get a light rust shade. Overdye ⅓ yard of this rust wool with 8/32 teaspoon of dry Mahogany and 2 tablespoons of a solution made with ½ teaspoon of Dark Brown dissolved in 1 cup of boiling water. Spot-dye the remaining rust wool with the Dark Brown solution, using approximately ½ cup of solution per ½ yard of wool. This spot-dyeing may be done in several batches,

Fireboard

Enlarge by 400 percent to
obtain 2-inch squares.

You must cut a piece of ¹/₂-inch plywood large enough to cover your fireplace opening and the back supports for the fireboard.

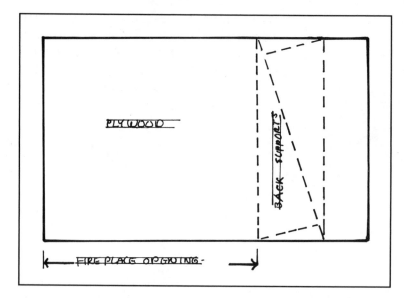

depending on the size of your pan. Each dye lot will be a little different, producing a variegated effect when the colors are used together.

Alternatives

The model was hooked with only four colors: gold, orange, light blue dip-dyed in rust, and brown-rust. The fireboard design was adapted from a nineteenth-century Italian inlaid decoration on the Orient Express, and the color scheme simulates the colors of the wood used in the original. Of course, more colors can be used for the flowers. Try repeating whatever color you choose for the filigree arch in the compote. Since there is substantial background, avoid using a single color for the background; mix several values to keep it interesting.

Getting Started

Measure your fireplace opening, adding 1 inch to the width and height. Then make your hooked piece this size. I suggest hooking the arch motif, the compote, and the flowers first. Cut sections of the spot-dyed background material for the light brown leaves and flowers, accenting the edges with orange where the motifs need to be separated from the background. Use some of the dark brown wool for the leaves behind the flowers. When hooking the blue flowers and the blue leaves, use the lightest sections of the dip-dyed pieces on the edges. The sections within the arch are filled with the evenly dyed dark brown wool. Using the rest of the spot-dyed wool, fill in the background, hooking diagonally from a central vertical and horizontal line to achieve a subtle, fanned background pattern. Draw guidelines on your backing to keep your rows straight. Go over your piece for holidays.

Getting Finished

Check the size of your finished piece against the plywood board and adjust the hooking if necessary. Apply Elmer's Glue-All ½ inch beyond the hooking, rubbing it well into the backing. Allow the glue to dry until it appears clear. Stain the back of the fireboard. Cover the front of

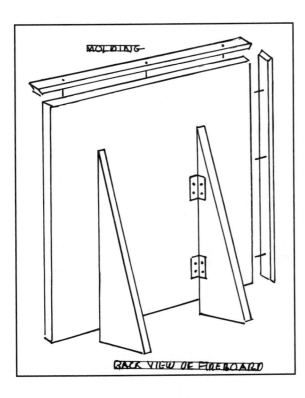

MOLDING

BACK VIEW OF FIREBOARD

The back of the fireboard is carefully finished. The back supports are attached to the back of the finished piece with hinges. The back supports are positioned so that the fireboard has a 1-inch clearance above the hearth.

the plywood with double-stick carpet tape, and position the hooked piece on it with the backing hanging over all the sides. Staple or tack the hooked piece around all the sides of the plywood. Attach mitered molding around all the sides of the board. Trim off the excess backing. Attach the back supports to the back of the finished piece with hinges, positioning them so that the fireboard has a 1-inch clearance above the hearth.

Wedding Rug

H & S

COME LIVE WITH ME
AND BE MY LOVE
AND WE WILL ALL THE
PLEASURES PROVE
NOVEMBER 14, 1959

This sampler-like wedding rug makes an unforgettable wedding gift. The opening lines of the Marlowe poem express the excitement and hope of a wedding day. The rug can be used during the ceremony for the bridal couple to stand on as they exchange their vows. Add the proper initials and date, and it becomes a treasured family heirloom.

Wedding Rug

Enlarge by 500 percent to
obtain 2-inch squares.

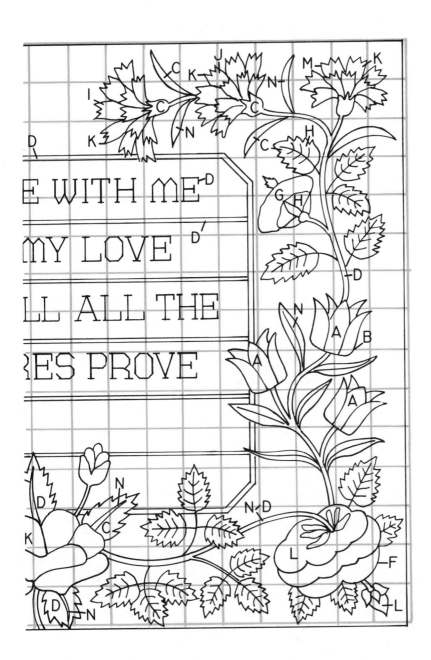

ABCDE
FGHIJK
LMNOP
QRSTU
VWXYZ
1234567890

Lettering for Wedding
Rug

Model size: 30 inches by 40 inches

Backing: 38-by-48-inch linen

Total wool amount: 45$\frac{1}{2}$ ounces of scraps and dyed wool

Strip width: #4 ($\frac{1}{8}$ inch)

Color amounts needed for hooking:

A.	Blue, light	1 ounce of scraps
B.	Blue, dark	$\frac{1}{2}$ ounce of scraps
C.	Blue-green, medium	1$\frac{1}{2}$ ounces of dyed wool
D.	Blue-green, dark	4 ounces ($\frac{1}{3}$ yard) of dyed wool
E.	Ecru	28 ounces (2$\frac{1}{3}$ yards) of dyed wool
F.	Gray-green	$\frac{1}{2}$ ounce of scraps
G.	Gold, light	$\frac{1}{2}$ ounce of scraps
H.	Gold, dark	1 ounce of dyed wool
I.	Pink	$\frac{1}{2}$ ounce of scraps
J.	Rose, light	1 ounce of dyed wool
K.	Rose, medium	1 ounce of dyed wool
L.	White	3$\frac{1}{2}$ ounces of scraps
M.	Wine	$\frac{1}{2}$ ounce of dyed wool
N.	Yellow-green	2 ounces of scraps

Materials needed for finishing:

4 yards of 1$\frac{1}{4}$-inch twill tape

4 yards of #100 cording (optional)

50 yards of triple-strand Persian yarn for whipping edge (optional)

Directions for Dyeing the Colors

You will need one package each of Blue, Buttercup, Cardinal, Ecru, Old Gold, Mahogany, Maroon, and Yellow Cushing Perfection Dyes.

Green Mountain Colors #12 (Blue-Green). Dissolve $\frac{1}{32}$ teaspoon Yellow, $\frac{2}{32}$ teaspoon Blue, and $\frac{4}{32}$ teaspoon Reseda in 1 cup boiling water. Over 4-by-14-inch white pieces, dye four pieces with 3 teaspoons each of the dye formula. Over $\frac{1}{3}$ yard white, use 14 tablespoons of a triple mixture of the formula given above.

Ecru. Over seven $\frac{1}{3}$-yard white pieces, use $\frac{1}{32}$ teaspoon dry Ecru per piece.

Green Mountain Colors #2 (Gold). Dissolve $\frac{1}{32}$ teaspoon Yellow, $\frac{4}{32}$ teaspoon Old Gold, and $\frac{1}{32}$ teaspoon Buttercup in 1 cup boiling water. Over 4-by-14-inch white pieces, dye three pieces with 3 teaspoons each of the dye formula and four pieces with 4 tablespoons each.

TOD #31/102 (Rose). Dissolve ½ teaspoon Cardinal, ¹/₁₆ teaspoon Maroon, and ¹/₁₆ teaspoon Mahogany in 1 cup boiling water. Over 3-by-12-inch white pieces, dye three pieces with ⅛ teaspoon each of the dye formula, three pieces with ½ teaspoon each, and one piece with 2 teaspoons each.

Alternatives

A wedding rug seems to demand a delicate coloring. If you are making the rug to use at the ceremony, a white, off-white, or very pale pastel background would be appropriate. Of course, the colors of the flowers and leaves may be varied, and they can be shaded rather than hooked in flat colors.

Getting Started

Before starting to hook, decide whether you wish to finish your project with twill tape or with a whipped edge. Both methods are described under Getting Finished. Start at any section desired. Always hook with the form, reinforcing the graceful curves of the vine and flowers. When hooking the quotation, be sure your loops are even and close. Snuggle the background around them so they appear straight and sharp. If the lines are ragged, your loops are not close enough. Of course, you can use a background hooked in horizontal rows throughout, but I repeated the curves of the motifs when hooking this section. After the rug is complete, check the back of your work for holidays.

Getting Finished

To finish your rug with twill tape, select 1¼-inch twill tape to match the edge of your rug, and machine stitch it around the edge *before* starting to hook. Machine zigzag two rows 1 inch beyond the pattern margin. As you hook the rug, work right up to the tape. After completing the rug, cut off the excess burlap beyond the zigzag stitching. Hem the tape over the backing edge. Using a damp towel, press your rug on the right side.

To finish your rug with a whipped edge, machine zigzag 1¼ inches beyond the last row of hooking and cut off the excess backing. Slip a piece of cording under the edge of the excess backing, pushing it right up against your last hooked row. Baste if you wish. Whipstitch this ridge. Using a tapestry needle threaded with a triple strand of Persian yarn, hide the knot in the cording. Bring the needle through to the front at the edge of the last row of hooking. Insert the needle from the back to the front again, bringing it through right next to the last stitch. Continue in this manner, completely covering the corded backing. Blind stitch twill tape over the narrow, exposed backing edge. Using a damp towel, press your piece on the right side.

Stair Runner

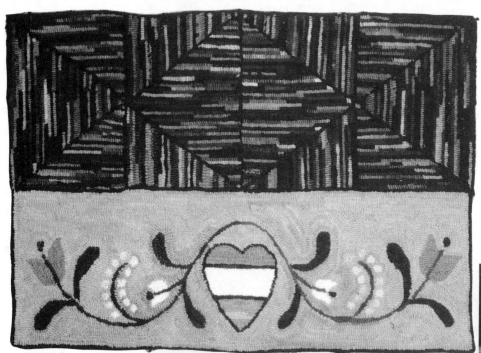

"Daddy, I'd like to hook a stair runner for my house. Could you design one for me?" The project was a natural for this book, and since Suzanne was going to hook it, everything fell into place. The four riser designs can be repeated to accommodate the number of risers in your staircase. Add initials and the date, so that future generations will give credit where credit is due.

Stair Runner

Enlarge by 460 percent to
obtain 2-inch squares.

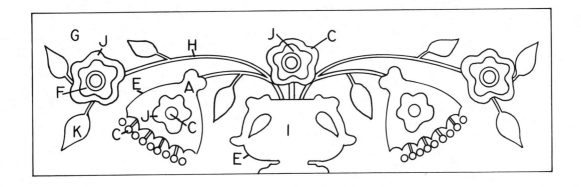

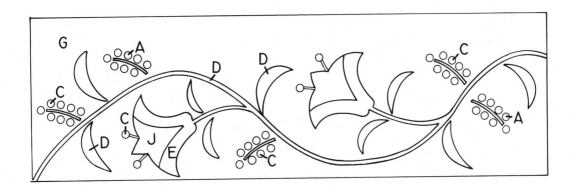

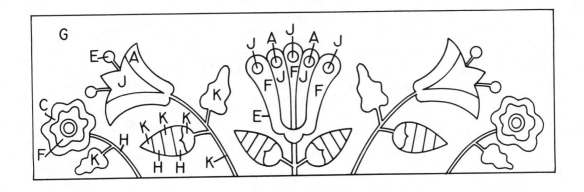

Model size: 8 1/2-by-28-inch Riser; 9 1/2-by-28-inch Tread

Backing: 24-by-36-inch linen for each tread and riser combined

Total wool amount for four risers and treads: 5 pounds of scraps and dyed wool

Strip width: #6 (3/16 inch)

Color amounts needed for hooking four risers:

A.	Blue	3 ounces
B.	Blue-green, dark	6 ounces
C.	Gold	2 ounces
D.	Jade	10 ounces
E.	Maroon	2 ounces
F.	Pink	1/2 ounce
G.	Rose	12 ounces of dyed wool
H.	Red-green plaid	1/2 ounce
I.	Tan	1/2 ounce
J.	White	2 ounces
K.	Yellow-green	1/2 ounce

Total amount of wool needed for hooking four treads in hit-or-miss fashion:
40 ounces. (The colors listed above should be repeated, except for the pink, blue, and tan, which should be repeated as darker values.)

Materials needed for finishing four treads and risers:

11 yards of 1 1/4-inch twill tape to match hooked edge

4 1/2 yards of #200 cording (optional)

75 yards of triple-strand Persian yarn (optional)

Directions for Dyeing the Pink Background

You will need one package each of Cardinal, Mahogany, and Maroon Cushing Perfection Dyes.

TOD #31/102 (Rose-Pink). Dissolve 1/2 teaspoon Maroon, 1/16 teaspoon Cardinal, and 1/16 teaspoon Mahogany in 1 cup boiling water. Using 2 teaspoons of this solution for each 1/3-yard white piece, dye four pieces.

TOD #31/103 (Rose-Brown). Dissolve 1/2 teaspoon Cardinal, 1/16 teaspoon Maroon, and 1/16 teaspoon Mahogany in 1 cup boiling water to create a second shade of rose. Dye four pieces, using 2 teaspoons of this solution per 1/3-yard white piece. Mixing these two shades makes an interesting background.

Alternatives

Of course, many different color schemes may be used for

these stair runners. The rose background can be replaced by a lighter or darker background with the motif colors adjusted as needed. The relationship of the riser to the tread is most important. The colors in the riser should be carried through in darker values in the tread, so that there is a feeling of unity throughout.

Getting Started

Measure the tread and riser sections of your stairs and adjust the pattern as necessary. Work each tread and riser as a unit to allow for easy adjustment. (The pattern will shrink slightly as you hook.) Begin with any section, hooking the motifs with the form and following these curves with the background rows. The hit-or-miss tread should be hooked in vertical and horizontal parallel rows for contrast. When the hooking is completed, check the back of your piece for holidays.

Getting Finished

Check the size of the tread-riser piece against the stair to be covered. Be sure to allow enough ease for padding under the tread section. Machine zigzag 1¼ inches beyond the last row of hooking and cut off the excess backing. Blind stitch twill tape over this backing edge. Or you may apply the tape to the bottom and top portions only, and whipstitch the side edges with a triple strand of matching Persian yarn. Slip a piece of cording under the edge of the excess backing, pushing it right up against your last hooked row. Baste if you wish. Whipstitch this ridge. Using a tapestry needle threaded with the Persian yarn, hide the knot in the cording. Bring the needle through to the front at the edge of the last row of hooking. Insert the needle from the back to the front again, bringing it through right next to the last stitch. Continue in this manner, completely covering the corded backing. Blind stitch twill tape over the narrow, exposed backing edge. Using a damp towel, press your piece on the right side.

For the best results in installing the stair runner, I suggest employing a professional carpet installer. Working together, you should be able to solve any fitting problems by adjusting the padding.

Tulip Bench Cover

This design, which captures the cheerful gaiety of a bed of spring tulips, was inspired by a gift of Dutch bulbs brought back from Holland by our daughter and her husband. Realistically shaded flowers against stylized leaves will make this bench cover a focal point in any room.

Model size: 18 inches by 36 inches

Backing: 28-by-52-inch linen

Total wool amount: 38½ ounces of #3 stripettes and dyed wool

Strip width: #3 (³/₃₂ inch)

Color amounts needed for hooking:

A.	Black-green #44	12 ounces (54 stripettes)
B.	Blue-green #25/2	½ ounce (2 stripettes)
C.	Blue-green #25/3	1 ounce (4 stripettes)
D.	Blue-green #25/4	1½ ounces (7 stripettes)
E.	Blue-green #25/5	6 ounces (30 stripettes)
F.	Red	17 ounces of dip-dyed wool (thirty-four 3-by-14-inch pieces)
G.	Yellow-green #28/3	½ ounce (2 stripettes)

Materials needed for finishing:

1¼ yards 45-inch muslin for pillow

8 pounds down/feathers for filling

⅝ yard backing fabric for bench cover

3¼ yards decorative braid

Directions for Dip-Dyeing Red for the Tulips

You will need one package each of Crimson, Garnet, and Yellow Cushing Perfection Dyes.

Green Mountain Colors #26 (Crimson). Dissolve ¹/₃₂ teaspoon Yellow, ¼ teaspoon Crimson, and ¹/₃₂ teaspoon Garnet in 1 cup boiling water. Dip-dye thirty-four 3-by-14-inch white strips starting with 2 tablespoons of formula. Replenish the dyebath with this amount of formula after every two strips. (See the section on dip-dyeing in the chapter "Collecting or Dyeing the Colors You Need.")

Alternatives

You can change the colors of the tulips, leaves, and background. To preserve the impact and clarity of the design, the tulips should be a single color, although the values could be slightly different. This design mimics a tulip border, which is striking because of its massed effect. The juxtaposition of carefully shaded forms against a simple background emphasizes the painterly shading that is so effectively done in hooking. This is not a design that is suitable for wide strips.

Tulip Bench Cover

Enlarge by 400 percent to
obtain 2-inch squares.

Tulip Bench Cover
(Detail)

Getting Started

Any section may be started. Always hook the details before doing the surrounding area. It is essential that your rows of hooking follow the form you are rendering. The arrows on the detail drawing indicate the working direction. When hooking the tulips, work each petal separately to preserve a layered appearance. A light edge will always overlap a darker, shadowed section. Study the black and white photograph as you work.

As a foil for the elaborately shaded tulips, the leaves have only enough shading to define their form and separate them slightly from the background. The viewer should see the tulips first, then discover the leaves. The background should be hooked following the shape of the tulips and leaves. A background hooked in parallel rows is not appropriate for this piece. In some areas, the dark leaves should almost disappear into the background.

When the hooking is complete, check the back of your piece for holidays.

Getting Finished

Machine zigzag 1 inch beyond the hooked edge and cut off the excess backing beyond. Using a damp towel, press the hooked piece on the right side. Using muslin, make a pillow with a 1½-inch boxing to match the size of the hooked top. (The boxing will give the pillow more dimension and fluffiness.) Fill the muslin pillow with down. Make a matching muslin boxed backing for the hooked bench cover. With right sides together, attach the backing on three sides to the hooked top. Insert the down-filled pillow and blind stitch the remaining side. Sew decorative braid to the edge to hide the joining.

Table of Weights and Measures

Rug hookers always want to know the amount of wool needed for a project, but, unfortunately, there are only approximate answers. Wool amounts are affected by strip

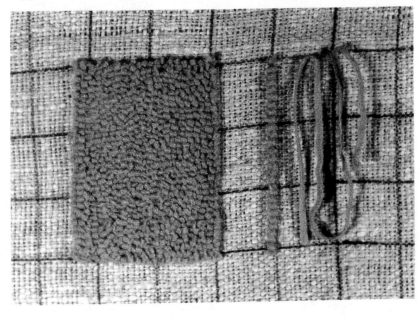

A #3 stripette is hooked on a 1-inch grid to illustrate the area that it will cover. A single hooked row and an unhooked strand are also shown. These narrow strips use the least amount of wool.

A #4 stripette is hooked on a 1-inch grid to illustrate the area covered. A single hooked row and an unhooked strand are also shown. The loops of #4 strips are slightly more pronounced than those of #3 strips. Also note that more wool is used.

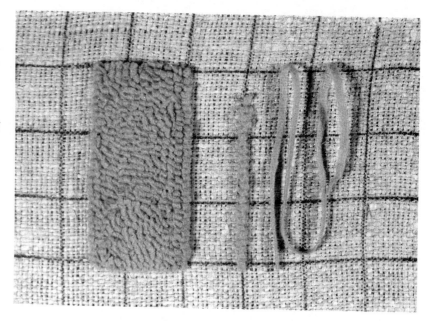

width, the length of tails, hooking styles, and the number of color changes. Wide strips (#6 or #8) consume more wool than #3 strips, because the loops will be higher and the pile will be thicker. Long tails, discarded at the beginning and end of rows, add up. Loops packed too tightly or made too far apart will also affect the wool count. An elaborately shaded piece, using many color values, will require more wool than a project with a simple color scheme.

The following table will help you estimate the amount of wool needed for a project. If the amount is not exact, you will understand why.

Yardage

One yard of wool flannel weighs 11 to 12 ounces.

Strip width	Wool amount	Coverage
#3	$1/3$ yard to $1/2$ yard	1 square foot
#4	$2/5$ yard to $5/8$ yard	1 square foot
#6	$1/2$ yard to $3/4$ yard	1 square foot

The smaller wool amounts would be appropriate when estimating the amount of wool needed to hook a plain

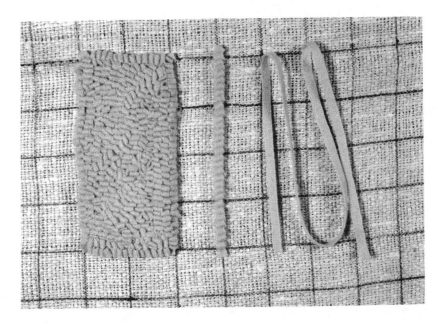

A #6 stripette is hooked on a 1-inch grid to illustrate the area covered. A single hooked row and an unhooked strand are also shown. Compare the prominent loops made with a #6.

background; the more generous amounts would accommodate several color changes.

Dismantled Garments

Garment	Wool amount
Boy's wool flannel jacket	12 ounces
Man's wool flannel jacket	1 pound
Man's wool flannel pants	12 ounces
Women's straight skirt	8 ounces

Precut Wool Strips (Stripettes)

#3 strip width equals one 3-by-12-inch flannel piece cut into 28 to 30 strands.

#4 strip width equals one 3-by-12-inch flannel piece cut into 25 strands.

#6 strip width equals one 3-by-12-inch flannel piece cut into 15 strands.

One #3 stripette will cover 6.75 square inches. One strip hooks a $2^{1}/_{2}$-inch row.

One #4 stripette will cover 4.5 square inches. One strip hooks a $2^{1}/_{4}$-inch row.

One #6 stripette will cover 8 square inches. One strip hooks a 4-inch row.

Glossary

Backing: The foundation material, or matrix, on which a hooked piece is worked. The backing may be cotton, burlap, or linen.

Bias: The diagonal line across a fabric.

Binding: The twill tape used to finish the edge of a hooked piece.

Burlap: The fabric most commonly used as the backing for hooked rugs.

Chroma: The brightness or intensity of a color.

Crosswise: The horizontal grain of fabric.

Cutter: A hand-operated machine for cutting wool strips for hooking.

Cutter head: A steel cylinder with multiple blades for cutting wool strips. Cutter heads are available in various sizes.

Dyebath: The mixture of water and dye in which fabric is dyed.

Fingering: A method of shading in which rows of one color are worked between rows of another.

Formula: The recipe for mixing several dyes; the dissolved mixture.

Hook: A steel shaft with a hook, similar to a crochet hook, set in a turned wooden handle. Hooks come in fine, medium, and coarse sizes.

Hit-or-miss: A term used to describe a rug or a section of a hooked piece made with multi-colored strips, usually hooked in parallel rows.

Holiday: The unhooked spaces found by checking the underside of a finished piece.

Hue: A technical term for color.

Mordant: A substance that fixes color in a textile.

Motif: In design, a feature, or part, of the whole decoration.

Pattern: An outline design printed on a backing.

Primitive hooking: Wide-strip hooking.

Sawtoothing: A method of shading in which loops of one row are zigzagged into loops of another.

Stripettes: A bunch of precut wool strips for hooking. They are available in #3, #4, and #6 widths.

Swatch: A dyed piece of wool from which strips are cut to use in hooking a rug, or several pieces of wool with related colors. Sometimes a swatch has six or eight different values of the same color. Sometimes it is spot-dyed or dip-dyed with a variety of colors.

Tapestry hooking: Hooking with fine strips, usually $3/32$-inch strips.

Transitional swatch: A group of six or eight wool pieces that range from the light of one color to the dark of another.

Value: The lightness or darkness of a color in relation to gray.

Sources of Supply

Catalogs and color cards are available as indicated, but they are not free. Please inquire about prices.

Appleton Krafts & Supplies, 50 Appleton Ave., S. Hamilton, MA 01982. Complete line of rug hooking supplies.

Ashworth, Anne, RD #1, Box 358, Randolph Center, VT 05061. Dye formula booklets, *Chroma Craft* and *Green Mountain Colors.*

Braid-Aid, 466 Washington St., Pembroke, MA 02359. Patterns, wool remnants, precut wool strips, and braiding supplies. Catalog.

Burlap 'n Rags, 52 Courtland St., Rockford, MI 49341. Supplies and kits for hooked rugs.

W. Cushing & Company/Joan Moshimer, P.O. Box 351, Kennebunkport, ME 04046. Manufacturers of Cushing Perfection Dyes. Color card. Patterns and supplies for rug hooking. Catalog.

Designs to Dream On, Jane McGown Flynn, Inc., P.O. Box 1301, Sterling, MA 01564. Complete line of supplies for rug hooking. Catalog.

DiFranza Designs, 25 Bow St., N. Reading, MA 01864. Patterns, custom design service, kits, and supplies for rug hooking. Outline-printed patterns from *Hooking Fine Gifts*. Catalog.

Dorr Mill Store, P.O. Box 88, Guild, NH 03754-0088. Wool by the yard, stripettes. Color card. Complete line of rug hooking supplies.

Ebi, Dotti, 501 Kingsbury, Dearborn, MI 48128. Booklet of formulas for spot dyeing, *Scraps and Spots*.

Fallier, Jeanne, The Rugging Room, P.O. Box 824, Westford, MA 01886. Patterns for hooked rugs. Repairing.

Forestheart Studio, 21 S. Carroll St., Frederick, MD 21701. Supplies for rug hooking, including linen backing.

Harry M. Fraser Co., Rt. 3, Box 254-1A, Stoneville, NC 27048. Manufacturer of cloth slitting machines. Complete line of supplies. Catalog.

Ginny's Gems, 5167 Robinhood Dr., Willoughby, OH 44094. Patterns, ProChem Dyes, and formula booklet. Catalog.

Jacqueline Designs, 237 Pine Point Rd., Scarborough, ME 04074. Patterns and supplies for hooked rugs. Catalog.

Janosh Industries, 39 Drexel Dr., Bay Shore, NY 11706. Premium quality cushioning products. (A good source for down for pillows.) Catalog.

New Earth Designs, Beaver Rd., RR #2, Box 301, La-Grangeville, NY 12540. Patterns and supplies for rug hooking. Catalog.

Patsy B, 18 Schank Rd., Holmdel, NJ 07733. Patterns for rug hooking. Catalog.

Pro Chemical & Dye, Inc., P.O. Box 14, Somerset, MA 02726. Acid dyes for wool and other commercial dyes. Catalog.

Rags to Rugs Craft Shoppe, 14 Eastmoor Dr., Truro, Nova Scotia B2N 2X3 Canada. Complete supplies for rug hooking.

Rug Hooking Magazine, Cameron & Kelker Sts., P.O. Box 15760, Harrisburg, PA 17105. Published five times a year, the magazine provides information on hooked rugs, how-tos, historical profiles, dye formulas, and patterns. $19.95 for one year's subscription ($24.95 in Canada, $35 overseas).

State Line Tack, Inc., P.O. Box 428, Route 121, Plaistow, NH 03065. Complete line of equestrian supplies, including Orvus WA Paste. Mail orders: 1-800-228-9208.

Sweet Briar Studio, 866 Main St., Hope Valley, RI 02832. Patterns and supplies for rug hooking. Catalog.

The Triple Over Dye Family, 187 Jane Dr., Syracuse, NY 13219. Booklet of formulas, swatches, dye spoons.

Index

Notes

Notes

Notes